TAMING AND TRAINING
MACAWS

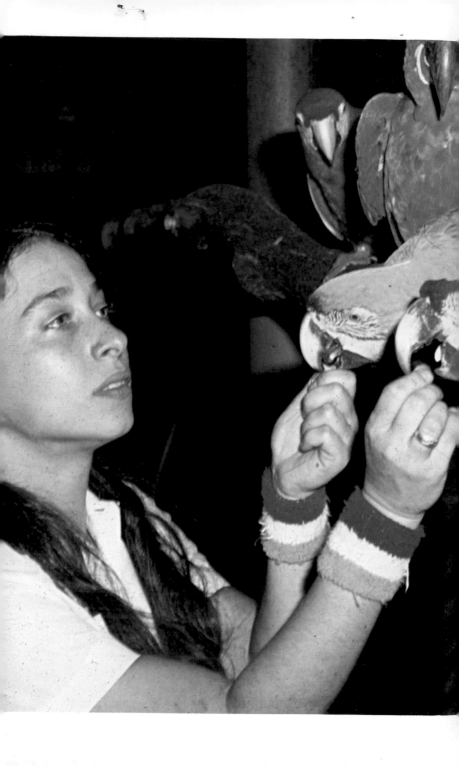

CONTENTS:

PHOTOGRAPHS: Title page shows the author with her trained macaws. Cover photography: Front cover shows a Brazilian Amazon Indian boy with his pet hyacinthine. The Indians use the feathers of large, colorful birds for decorations. The back cover shows the author at work in the Parrot Jungle in Miami, Florida, where she trains large parrots.

The front endpapers show the author treating her tamed and trained macaws to peanuts as a reward for their successful performance of a complicated routine. The back endpapers show the author with her trained macaw "playing dead" by lying on its back in her hand. All photos not otherwise credited were taken by Dr. Herbert R. Axelrod.

All the macaws shown with the author and referred to as "her" birds are, of course, the property of the Parrot Jungle and are on display at the Parrot Jungle in Miami. Both the author and publisher are deeply indebted to the Parrot Jungle for their fine cooperation.

t.f.h.

© 1979 by T.F.H. Publications, Inc.

ISBN 0-87666-884-8

Distributed in the UNITED STATES by T.F.H. Publications, Inc., 211 West Sylvania Avenue, Neptune City, NJ 07753; in CANADA by H & L Pet Supplies Inc., 27 Kingston Crescent, Kitchener, Ontario N2B 2T6; Rolf C. Hagen Ltd., 3225 Sartelon Street, Montreal 382 Quebec; in ENGLAND by T.F.H. (Great Britain) Ltd., 11 Ormside Way, Holmethorpe Industrial Estate, Redhill, Surrey RH1 2PX; in AUSTRALIA AND THE SOUTH PACIFIC by T.F.H. (Australia) Pty. Ltd., Box 149, Brookvale 2100 N.S.W., Australia; in NEW ZEALAND by Ross Haines & Son, Ltd., 18 Monmouth Street, Grey Lynn, Auckland 2 New Zealand; in SINGAPORE AND MALAYSIA by MPH Distributors Pte., 71-77 Stamford Road, Singapore 0617; in the PHILIPPINES by Bio-Research, 5 Lippay Street, San Lorenzo Village, Makati, Rizal; in SOUTH AFRICA by Multipet Pty. Ltd., 30 Turners Avenue, Durban 4001. Published by T.F.H. Publications Inc., Ltd., the British Crown Colony of Hong Kong. THIS IS THE 1983 EDITION.

TAMING AND TRAINING
MACAWS

by **RISA TEITLER**
PROFESSIONAL TRAINER

A pair of macaws preening above. On the facing page is the red and yellow macaw, *Ara macao*. The Brazilian Indians call this macaw "ara," thus the derivation of the scientific name for the genus.

Above: Unless you clip a macaw's wing, it can fly and perhaps escape or injure itself. Clipping also greatly aids in taming, and the bird can easily be trained to climb onto a suitable stick (right) for further domestication.

Introduction

Taming and Training Macaws is for people who desire to keep a macaw for a pet. Because of their size and intelligence, macaws require much more training than the average caged bird. The book is devoted entirely to information that will help macaw owners tame and train their pets.

Information on breeding and physiology was excluded from the text in an effort to give maximum space to the taming and training sections. Even so, there is still more on taming and behavior modification programs that could have been included.

The first aid and illness section is intentionally short. It is hoped that the macaw owner will seek out a specialist in avian medicine to assist with any health problems encountered.

Appreciate your new macaw and be absolutely sure to train it.

Risa Teitler

Taming and Training Macaws

The above photo shows the author with Nubbins, one of the Parrot Jungle's free flying macaws. These free-flying macaws could fly back to Brazil if they so desired, but they live freely at the Parrot Jungle in Miami. The macaw to the right belongs to the Honolulu Bird Park. It has been trained to push a toy car.

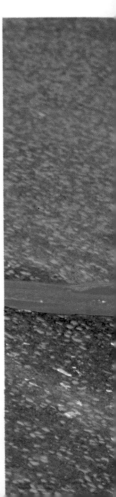

10

ABOUT MACAWS IN GENERAL

There are three genera of macaws and many different species. The most common macaws, the scarlet, green-winged, military and blue and gold, belong to the genus *Ara*. The hyacinth macaw, Lear's macaw and the glaucous macaw belong to the genus *Anodorhynchus;* all have dark blue plumage and bright yellow skin around the eyes and the lower mandibles. The third genus, *Cyanopsitta,* has one member only, the very rare Spix's macaw.

This text will mention the *Ara* species more frequently than the other two genera, because the *Ara* species are the most common macaws in captivity. The hyacinth macaw, although less common as a caged pet, will also be the subject of some special remarks.

All species of macaws occur in South and Central America and Mexico. A few species, now extinct, once inhabited the islands of the Caribbean. Macaws range in size from very small (the red-shouldered macaw is just 30 cm in length) to extremely large (100 cm for the magnificent hyacinth). All *Ara* species have conspicuous patches of bare skin on the face, although some species, such as the military, green-winged and blue and gold, have bands of short feathers striping the facial skin. All macaws have long tapering tail feathers and display brilliantly colored plumage. Some of the feathers are tiny, whereas others, such as the heavy flight feathers of the wing and tail, are very large. Beneath the colored outer feathers is a thick layer of gray down; this layer provides ample insulation from cold weather and helps regulate the body temperature. Some birds appear to have eyelashes. In reality these "eyelashes" are specially structured feathers. There is no sexual dimorphism in any of the species, and immature birds resemble the parents.

Mandibles are made of hard keratin and may be beige, black, grayish or two-toned. The upper mandible is solid and tapers to a point on the end; the lower has a curved edge and forms the floor of the oral cavity. Stories relating to the amount of pressure in the bite of macaws do not exaggerate when they tell of individuals breaking broom handles in half. It has been my experience that many macaws occupy themselves by crushing coral or granite rock when made available. Indeed the macaws are capable of inflicting serious wounds if handled improperly, but for the most part they are docile, gentle birds that will not bite unless provoked.

The legs and feet are scaled and may be black, gray or beige, depending upon the species. Some individuals lose the dark coloration on the feet and legs as they grow older or as a result of poor nutrition or illness. Like other parrots, the macaws have a four-toed foot, two toes facing to the front and two to the rear. The claws are strong and pointed, made of the same material as the beak. In battle the claws are used as weapons very effectively. Claws may be grayish black or beige.

The disposition of the birds varies from individual to individual and not as a function of species. Some macaws can be quite aggressive, but the majority are docile creatures. You may encounter an extremely nervous macaw—certainly some that I have known were emotionally disturbed. The point here is that no one group of macaws is more gentle or more aggressive than any other group. Do not listen to people who label one species gentle and another nasty. The labelers have not had ample experience handling macaws or they would refrain from such labeling.

Macaws are long-lived birds, with a life expectancy of approximately 50 to 65 years. This is a conservative estimate, but the stories about macaws living to 100 years and more would have to have documented proof to convince me. A 60-year-old macaw is an old bird. Some individuals may live into their 70's, while others may not make it to 50. A great deal depends upon genetic disposition and the general health of the individual.

There are distinct stages in the life cycle of macaws: infancy, childhood, adolescence, young adulthood, maturity, middle age and old age. These are not rigid stages. A five-year-old does not suddenly leap from childhood to adolescence; the changes are gradual but definite. Macaws are reproductively mature for many years, beginning at about 6 to 8 years of age. Some mature more quickly than others. They have been known to reproduce in their 30's, and there are a few reports of birds rearing young at 40 years of age. As macaws grow older they tend to become sedate individuals with definite habit patterns. They like a set routine. Late in life they may suffer from many of the same symptoms of old age as humans—arthritis, obesity, cataracts, hearing loss and hardening of the arteries.

Macaws can make excellent pets if handled properly. In the wrong environment or with the wrong people, though, macaws can be very difficult to deal with and even dangerous. I do not recommend pet macaws in a household with young children. Macaws tend to equate themselves with children, or they are very egocentric creatures. They may become jealous of the attention that the human youngsters get. Little children have a way of getting their fingers into the powerful beaks of macaws. Depending upon the individual bird's personality, this may or may not be a tragedy. If you absolutely *must* have a macaw in a house with young children, take precautions to protect both the children and the bird. Keep the bird out of the child's reach at all times. It only takes one bite to severely damage a child's tiny fingers. Better yet, wait until the kids are older before getting a macaw.

To be a good pet, a macaw must have at least one dedicated trainer. Macaws, like children, must be trained to live in human society. This sort of behavioral training is an absolute necessity or the bird will eventually be a nuisance rather than an asset to the owner. One of the fastest ways I know of to lose a good friend is to have that friend bitten by your macaw. And don't forget the abundance of noise that a macaw can make if it feels like it. You really need good neighbors if you plan to keep a macaw in a residential neighborhood. Besides the noise, macaws can think up all sorts of ways to get your attention. Truly, they do have a

The author with her macaws. Not only are macaws easily tamable and trainable, but they readily interbreed and extremely colorful hybrids result.

The resulting hybrids are not sterile and they also can be interbred with results which almost defy a determination of their heritage.

tremendous craving for attention and a great variety of attention-getting behavior. From the standpoint of the bird trainer, macaws' desire for attention is fortunate; without it, they'd be much less trainable.

With this in mind, consider also the time investment that you must make if you are to successfully keep a macaw for a pet. Time to accomplish the initial taming is just the beginning. Once the bird is tame, it requires interaction with you on a daily basis to develop its personality in the right direction. You must give the macaw plenty of guidance or its personality may develop most undesirably. It is a common mistake that people cannot conceive of a bird having a personality. Consider that the macaw is a long-lived, intelligent bird with an emotional makeup similar to that of humans. It is a basic function of life that the personality must develop to allow the bird to cope with its environment. If you provide the proper guidance the bird will develop amicably. If not, you will probably want to get rid of the bird after a few years, for you will neither understand its behavior nor be able to effectively change it for the better.

You will also find yourself devoting a great deal of time to cleaning up the bird's cage and accessories and the room that the cage sits in. Macaws are messy eaters and tend to throw their toys around. Another problem that you will encounter is how to go away on vacation and provide adequate care for the macaw. Your neighbor may have had lots of parakeets, but caring for a macaw requires more than parakeet experience. You cannot leave a macaw with just anyone; most people are better equipped to handle your child.

The last major consideration that you must make before buying a macaw is the birds' natural tendency to chew things up. They can be very destructive chewers. If you have wood furniture or paneling, beware. Leather furniture, shoes and pocketbooks are not safe either. Paintings and picture frames may meet a sad demise once a macaw becomes interested in them. I know of very little that a macaw will refrain from chewing. I had one break every weld on a wrought iron cage for entertainment while I was at work. Even when the cage was wired up, he broke the door off its hinges. With some macaws, only a very heavy metal cage will do. Others are content to chew wood if you provide it regularly and in quantity.

In the right environment, with a highly motivated trainer, a macaw can make a fabulous pet, more interesting than a dog and capable of doing more—and a more satisfying companion.

Some macaws are tamed fairly easily, while others can be very difficult. The great majority can be tamed if the trainer has the correct approach, a workable behavior program and enough time to devote to the task. If you lack the time to tame the bird, you lack the time to follow through even if someone else does the taming for you. In this case, don't buy a macaw. Both you and the bird will be unhappy. If you do have the time and personal discipline to tame the bird you will probably be able to teach it to speak and do a few tricks. A motivated trainer can accomplish unbelievable results with a good macaw. The birds' natural desire for attention and their gregarious natures make macaws about the most trainable of all parrots. (Macaws and cockatoos are on a par when it comes to trainability.)

The capacity for speech varies from bird to bird. Although all macaws have the potential for speech, there are many contributing factors that will determine an individual bird's progress. Some birds, like some people, have more sensitive hearing than others. These birds are more likely to duplicate sound accurately. Some birds, although they hear very well, have poor voice quality. This is probably the result of physiological factors such as the vocal cords, the oral cavity and the tongue. These birds often try very hard to duplicate your sound, but they just don't sound like the human voice. Unlike the Amazon parrots, which copy the sound of the trainer's voice exactly, macaws have their own natural pitch and tone. The same word ("Hello," for example) taught by the same trainer to three or four different macaws will sound different when each bird says it.

Occasionally you may encounter a macaw with such a good voice quality that it will amaze you. These birds are often capable of acquiring large vocabularies if given enough consistent training. Macaws love to talk—to you, to themselves, to other birds and animals. A pet macaw is a happier bird if he can talk to you.

The ears of macaws are small openings on the sides of the head, covered by feathers. They have a wide range of hearing from low frequency to high frequency sounds. Macaws appear to hear warning cries from other birds before we do, for their hearing is more acute than ours.

Intelligence varies considerably from bird to bird. Some are so smart that they learn with a minimum of guidance. Others seem to understand nothing and are unable to learn the simplest tricks. Some are even unaware of their own safety; these are really dumb birds, but they are not often encountered.

Macaws have excellent eyesight. They can focus on both close and distant objects. They see colors and can easily distinguish shapes (i.e. circles, stars and squares).

It is reasonable to assume, based on macaws' excellent data processing equipment, eyesight and hearing, that macaws are extremely intelligent.

Macaws are very difficult to breed in captivity. Some birds appear to

1

2

1. The bird on the left is a natural (not a hybrid) blue and gold macaw, while the bird being playfully "kissed" is an orange hybrid. 2. The author training a hybrid macaw which resulted from a cross of a blue and gold with green-winged macaw. 3. The author in the training cage with a military x scarlet macaw on her shoulder and the normal scarlet macaw on her arm. The birds are very gentle with the author and rarely bite or scratch her.

19

lose interest in reproduction even if a companion of the opposite sex is present. Many macaws seem more motivated toward having a good relationship with another bird or even a person than they are toward breeding. They do not rear large numbers of young, as do the smaller parrots, and they may not nest every year even once they begin breeding. The average number of young per nest is two. Some pairs raise three successfully, while others raise only one.

The dietary requirements of macaws are extensive. You must provide ample amounts of fresh fruit and vegetables in addition to a good quality of sunflower seed and raw peanuts. Supplements to the diet in the form of vitamins and minerals must be provided on a daily basis. See the section on "Feeding" for more detailed information.

Macaws are very energetic birds and require a great deal of room in which to exercise. For this reason it is necessary to provide a macaw with *both* a stand and a large cage. Birds that live on an open stand 24 hours a day do not have ample room to exercise. Macaws must be able to climb around to remain in good condition. Birds that live in a cage 24 hours a day may have enough room to climb, but they usually lack the opportunity to flap their wings and stretch out comfortably. Macaws have a high activity level and must have ample time and space to exercise if they are to remain healthy.

Generally speaking, macaws are hardy birds. If fed and housed properly they may never become ill. With good food and clean surroundings, most macaws can throw off illness and injury with little or no after-effects. Some individual macaws, like some people, may always catch whatever bug is in the air. Obviously these birds require special care to remain in good health. Some macaws may even develop allergies, but this is not a common concern with captive birds.

Cold weather does not harm a healthy well fed macaw, but care should be taken to protect it from temperatures below 40 degrees Fahrenheit. Some people winter their macaws out of doors even in the snow, but these birds must be provided with shelter from the elements, and of course they have to be acclimated to living outside before the winter arrives. It is best to place a macaw in an outdoor aviary in the spring to allow it time to molt in the proper feathers and build up necessary fat to protect it from the cold.

Occasionally you may see a handicapped or imperfect macaw for sale. Such birds are usually lower in price than perfect birds, as they should be. However, a handicapped macaw can make as good a pet as a perfect bird. Obviously it will require more specialized care and handling. The most common handicapping conditions are blindness in one eye and a badly healed broken bone in the leg or wing. The limb may angle out from the torso unnaturally and be unsightly, but generally the bird will compensate for these disabilities very well. Some macaws receive injuries during the importation process or after they arrive in the importing country. One missing toe or claw is not a major handicap, but two or more missing toes may be. Again, use your common sense before purchasing the bird. If the price is greatly reduced you may be getting yourself a potentially good pet and in addition will be doing the macaw a great service. However, never buy an imperfect macaw at a premium price.

It is best to buy only one macaw if you plan to tame it for a pet. Two birds housed together are much more difficult to tame unless you have adequate experience. If two birds are your heart's desire, buy them one at a time and tame the first before you buy the second.

For people who want to display a macaw in their shops, offices or gardens, there are additional considerations. It is not adequate to tame the bird to one person or one sex if it will be exposed to many people of both sexes. Macaws are usually displayed on open perches. It is imperative that these birds be trained to remain sitting on the stand for long periods of time. They must also be trained to a stick to make them easily retrievable if they should be scared or chased off the stand. It is advisable to arm-train these macaws and teach them to eat from your hand, for people tend to attempt to pick up the bird and touch it or feed it when they see it on an open perch. They don't seem to know that the bird can bite them. For the bird's own safety, you must pay attention to its training if you plan to display it.

Handicapped or lame birds are cheaper than a perfect specimen, and many make excellent pets.

The author with a trained hyacinth macaw. Macaws are hardy birds. If fed and housed properly, they may well outlive their owner.

Cold weather usually does not harm a healthy macaw, as their feathers are excellent insulation, especially if they are kept out of a breeze at night.

The author with a third generation hybrid. Though macaws do breed intermittently, they are not prolific producers of chicks.

Ann Simington owns a petshop and sells birds. She obviously loves and understands birds and would have the kind of petshop from which a macaw could be purchased with confidence. Photo by Terry Junkins.

How to Buy a Macaw

There are very strict laws in most countries pertaining to the importation and export of most exotic birds and monkeys. Before buying a macaw from anyone except your local petshop be sure that the bird is "legal" and that you are allowed to own it. Confiscation of illegal pets usually results in their being turned over to "humane" societies.

Most prospective buyers seek out a retailer who handles the type of bird they have in mind. This is fine if the retailer is knowledgeable and can provide you with adequate information on the care, feeding and taming of macaws or offers a bird already tame for sale. If you find a macaw in a pet shop chained to a stand, it is an indication that the proprietor knows very little about macaws or just doesn't care. If the bird is tame and the price is right, go ahead and liberate the creature. Take it home and remove the chain immediately. Train the bird to sit on the stand without the leg chain. He'll love you for it.

Macaws that are caged in pet shops are usually very wild, frightened birds. This does not mean that they can't be tamed, it just means the retailer could not accomplish the task. If the macaw is said to be tame, ask the retailer to demonstrate by handling the bird. A tame macaw should step onto your arm without biting or hesitating. It should take seed from your hand gently. It should remain sitting on your arm for at least a few minutes before wanting to return to the stand.

1

2

3

1. The author holds out the wing of a third generation hybrid. Birds with this coloration do not appear in nature. 2. Trainers of macaws, like the author, require a love and dedication that cannot be measured in hours or money. Each bird is an individual requiring different handling from the next macaw to come along. 3. A military macaw, *Ara militaris mexicana,* cracking a sunflower seed to remove the meat.

When buying from a retail pet shop, use your eyes and your nose to determine whether the shop is worth patronizing. If you can smell the birds, their droppings or their feed, you might be better off looking elsewhere. (But don't be too quick to condemn a shop after only one visit; the day you came might not be representative of the shop's normal pattern.) Inquire whether the shop can recommend a professional trainer if their macaws are not tame. Ask for the available literature (other than this book, of course) regarding the care and taming of macaws. If there is no additional literature available and the macaw is a good one, go ahead and buy it, but always be certain to obtain and study the literature on macaws when you purchase one.

A well stocked bird shop will offer a high-quality feed and the important mineral and vitamin supplements that you must give the macaw to keep it in good condition. If the shop does not house its macaws in adequate cages, ask to look through cage catalogs, for you may want the shop to order a cage for you.

There are other outlets besides pet retailers that sell macaws. Some importers also sell their birds to the public at wholesale prices. Most of the importers will not sell a single bird, for their business is in quantity sales, but if you live in a city that has ports of entry for exotic birds and quarantine facilities, go ahead and give them a call. Inquire whether they will sell a single bird to a private individual. If so, go over and look at the merchandise. Even if you decide not to buy from the wholesaler, it is educational to visit. Wholesalers can offer you a larger selection of macaws to choose from at a lower price, but the birds are usually caged in large flights, making it difficult for the inexperienced buyer to choose a good bird.

You may find a private person with a macaw for sale. Usually these are individuals who bought a macaw and were unable to tame it or unable to live with it. By all means, go over and see the bird. Bring cash with you, for the price may come down if you offer cash. Keep in mind that a macaw that has lived for many years with a family has developed behavior patterns that will be difficult to break. If the bird exhibits good behavior, you can consider buying it. If it doesn't and you still want to buy the bird, be prepared to put in many hours retraining the macaw. Retraining is possible, but it takes a lot of time, a highly motivated trainer and a sensible training program.

Pet macaws also are occasionally available from private breeders. Domestically bred macaws are usually more expensive, but they can be well worth the extra expense. They are usually in better feather and more acclimated to living with people. Many breeders offer a limited number of hand-reared young for sale. Breeders are hard to locate but well worth the search.

Some retailers offer to get a macaw even though they may not have one for sale in the shop. Be aware that you will be purchasing the bird sight unseen. Make sure that your deposit (if required) is refundable if the bird is an unholy mess. Remember, however, that most macaws come through quarantine with their feathers broken off. The long tail is usually absent or shabby at best. Often the wing feathers are clipped off or broken. As long as the bird does not appear to have chewed its feathers it is purchasable. If there are patches of feathers missing from the breast or the back or the neck, or if all of the feathers on both wings and the tail are broken off short, it is reasonable to assume that the bird has been chewing its feathers. Sometimes this behavior is caused by excessive stress, poor diet or crowded quarters. In some cases feather chewing is an acquired habit—a very difficult habit to break. It is not wise to buy a macaw with chewed-up feathers.

It is possible to buy a macaw in South America or Mexico. Be certain that you understand and abide by the laws that regulate the importation of exotic birds or you may find yourself in a bind at the border. If you are planning a vacation to South America or Mexico and you would like to bring back a bird, check on the law before you go. You will probably have to have the bird in your possession for 90 days or more on the other side of the border, and you will have to provide documents attesting to the macaw's health, origin and destination. You will also be required to keep the macaw in a 30-day home quarantine if you are able to get it across the border. Some South American countries may have additional laws regulating the export of macaws. Make sure that you know all the laws concerning your endeavor before attempting to bring a macaw home with you.

Really, it doesn't pay to try to scrimp on the purchase price of the bird you buy if your scrimping results in getting you a sick or maladjusted bird. Certainly it doesn't pay to try to save if your efforts force you into dealing with unscrupulous fly-by-nights and extra-legal operators. In the main, established pet shops will be the best source, especially for potential buyers who don't have access to private breeders.

A scarlet macaw with a closed eyelid. Many veterinarians now specialize in large birds (think of turkeys and chickens!), and they should be consulted if you feel you have a problem.

Choosing A Healthy Macaw

It takes two people to cut or file a macaw's claws. One person holds the macaw firmly, immobilizing the beak and the feet, while the second person does the grooming.

No matter where you buy the macaw and regardless of its price, you should look for indications of good health. The eyes should be clear and bright, free of discharge, cloudiness, irritation and swelling. The eye rings should have no scratches, open wounds, scales or scabs. The eye lids must be open (not closed) or the bird may have an eye problem. The nares (nasal passages) must be free of dirt and discharge, regularly shaped and positioned properly in the facial mask.

Facial skin should be smooth and even in color and free of sores (a scratch is not a sore). White skin with pink patching is not normal. Unless it is apparent that the macaw is blushing from excitement, pink or red patches on the facial skin represent skin problems.

The mandibles must fit together properly and have no obvious signs of wear. Fungal infections of the beak matter are not uncommon in exotic birds. If you suspect a fungal infection of the beak matter, do not buy the bird.

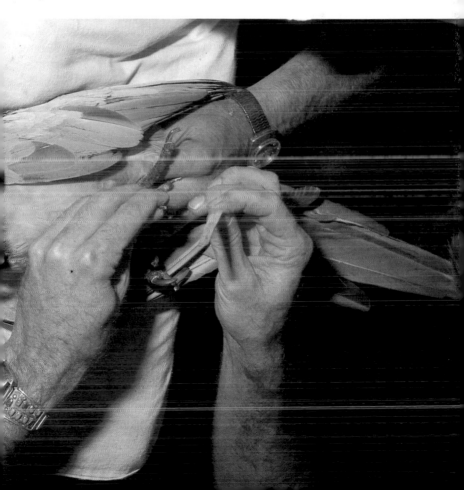

Scales of the feet and legs must be clean and even. Wounds on the legs and feet are undesirable. The feet should have equal gripping strength and even heat. Having even heat means that both feet have the same temperature to the touch. One hot and one cold foot can indicate the presence of either an infection or a circulatory malfunction. A healthy macaw should have four toes and four claws on either foot. A missing toe or claw is no serious disability. Do not buy a bird with a recent unhealed injury to the toe or claw.

As mentioned earlier, the heavy flight feathers are often in bad shape when the birds get through quarantine. Unless there is evidence of chewing, don't worry about broken flight feathers. It may take months before the old feathers have molted out and new ones grow, but broken feathers are the usual result of cramped quarters. If one wing or both wings droop badly or stick out from the body at an angle, the bird has some sort of problem and should not be purchased. If there are lumps, bumps or sores at the base of the flight feathers, think carefully before buying the macaw. Lumps may indicate follicle damage in the form of ingrown feathers. Although this condition can be alleviated with proper treatment, it is unwise to purchase a macaw that has obvious follicle damage.

Although the heavy flight feathers of the wing and tail may be broken, do not buy a macaw with patches of body feathers missing. This indicates some other problem, either feather chewing or possibly a skin problem. Exposed blood feathers on the end of the wing are a serious hazard when attempting to tame the new macaw, so be aware that special care must be taken with these individuals, but don't reject a bird for having blood feathers on the end of the wing if it passes all of the other criteria for good health.

The vent must be clean. A soiled or distended vent indicates a digestive disorder. Do not purchase a macaw with an obviously soiled or distended vent. Macaws sometimes suffer from hemorrhoids, so a distended vent can be a sign of internal pressure.

The droppings must be of solid form and have both dark green and white matter. Yellowish, orange, all-white, black or watery droppings indicate illness. Do not purchase a macaw with unhealthy droppings, for the droppings are the best indicators of health.

Whenever possible, have the seller hold the macaw for you to examine. Most sellers are not experienced bird handlers, so when you find one who is willing to hold the bird, take advantage of it. Feel the bird's breast. There should be plenty of meat on either side of the breastbone. If you can see and feel that the breastbone sticks out and has no meat on either side of it, do not buy the bird. Thin birds have not been eating well, possibly because they're suffering from illness.

Use these same criteria for choosing a good breeding bird, but add the following. Look for a large bird in good proportion. Try to determine the age and sex of the bird. It doesn't make sense for you to buy two birds of unknown age and sex if you plan to try a breeding experiment. Always buy perfect birds for breeding. Imperfect birds make fine pets and may be good parents, but it is important for breeding birds to have all of their toes, claws and senses. Rearing young in captivity is hard enough without adding other obstacles.

CHOOSING A MACAW FOR TAMABILITY

Once you have determined that the prospective macaw is active, alert and healthy, look for signs of tamability. Make eye contact with the macaw. If he looks you straight in the eye the bird has self-confidence and is a good candidate for taming. Macaws that actively avoid your stare are insecure birds. Move slowly in front of the macaw, from side to side. Does the bird follow your movement or does it scream and yell? A screaming macaw is afraid of your movement, but if it maintains eye contact with you, don't let the screaming bother you. Once the macaw is used to its new surroundings the screaming will abate. If it screams *and* refuses to maintain eye contact, reconsider the purchase.

Slowly lift your arm and move it very slowly back and forth in front of the bird. A macaw that follows the movement of your arm and shows no fear of it is a steady bird and a good prospect for taming and training.

Talk to the macaw. If it cocks its head and listens to your voice, it is showing interest. Naturally, a macaw that is housed in a cage with many other birds is not going to be overly interested in what you have to say. But a single macaw should show some interest in the sounds that you make if it is an intelligent bird.

When "interviewing" your potential pet macaw, consider the screaming when it also refuses to maintain eye contact with you.

Keeping a macaw at home usually requires you to adjust the house a bit! A part of the house must be set aside for the bird's cage and stand. The ideal setup is an outside aviary (shown below) but this too has many problems for the aviculturist.

Environment

To keep a macaw as a pet inside the house requires that you adjust the household somewhat. A large part of at least one room in the house must be set aside for the parrot's cage and a regular bird stand area. This does not mean that you should always leave the stand in one spot. It is best to be able to transport the bird stand from room to room and even outside to give your pet a secure perch wherever it is in the house. However, you will have to have a place to keep the stand when it is not in use and the bird is in its cage. Many people, feeling that a cage is not necessary, plan to keep the macaw on a stand most of the time. They feel that this is a more humane way to keep a macaw, giving it total liberty. I disagree. Although the macaw should be left out on the open perch for at least a couple of hours each day (the more free time the better), the bird should not have to remain on the stand 24 hours a day. This is far too restrictive for a young, healthy macaw. Macaws spend most of their day climbing around for exercise and entertainment. A well designed spacious macaw cage is the perfect place for the bird to climb around. The cage is the safest place for the bird to roost and gives it a feeling of security. You do not necessarily have to feed and water the macaw inside the cage. If your bird stand has sufficiently large easy-to-clean cups, go ahead and use them.

The best environment for a pet macaw inside the home includes a secure cage and a sturdy, transportable bird stand. The bird should be left caged if you plan to leave it alone in the house for long periods of time. A macaw can do extensive damage to the inside of a home in just a couple of hours. Leaving the bird at liberty for long periods of time is an invitation to disaster. The bird may find its way to an electric cord as it chews its way through your home. So even if you aren't concerned with the destructive potential of the macaw, think about its safety. Regard the macaw the same way you'd regard a child. Don't leave any dangerous chemicals or objects in any accessible spot.

No matter where the cage is in the house, protect the macaw from air conditioning drafts and dry radiator heat. If you live in a cold climate, try to winter the bird away from doors and windows. Although some birds become conditioned to very cold temperatures if they live outside, indoor pets do not have the benefit of outside conditioning.

People that entertain often should be careful to protect their pet from smoke-filled rooms. Keep the cage in a well ventilated place.

A large patio is a very good place for the macaw cage. Do not use a screened patio as the bird's aviary. A macaw will go through screening in seconds. The outdoor aviary must be thoughtfully constructed to provide easy cleaning, ample exercise space and safeguards against rodent entry. In addition, the structure must be able to withstand the chewing activity of the average macaw. Chain link fencing is perfect for an outdoor flight cage, but unfortunately it is very expensive. When using chain link you must also use an outer sheet of smaller wire mesh to keep pests out. Squirrels, chipmunks, raccoons, rats and mice must be kept from eating the bird's daily ration and drinking its water. Their very presence in the flight can cause the bird to injure itself by flying into wire if it is wakened suddenly in the middle of the night.

Also keep in mind that other inhabitants of the community are going to see a macaw outside in your yard or on your unscreened patio. Dogs, cats and children can be hazardous to the health of your macaw. On the other hand, your macaw could be the main reason that your neighbor stops talking to you, especially if it screams often. Loud birds usually need to have walls around them to muffle the sound and preserve good neighbor relations.

The indoor cage should be large enough for the bird to stretch out its wings without bending its feathers. If the cage is small the bird will never have a beautiful long tail. Even tall narrow cages will not allow the macaw to grow a long tail. The bird must be able to turn around without constantly brushing its tail against the wire. Wrought iron cages are good for indoors and usually attractive. These are expensive cages, but you cannot house a macaw in a standard parrot cage. Don't even try. Some pet supply stores carry collapsible nickel-plated cages of good dimensions. Some of these are very sturdy when put together properly and are much easier to fit through your front door than wrought iron.

Many macaws are prone to opening up their cage doors whenever they feel like going out. These birds must be kept in by placing a lock on the door when you are not at home.

An adequate indoor macaw cage is at least 5½ feet high and 3 feet square. These are the *smallest* acceptable dimensions. The macaw is well able to use additional space and is happier in a larger cage. Birds that have the 5½ x 3 feet cage need plenty of time out on the open perch for exercise. The commercially made macaw cage is better inside the home than a homemade cage. Macaws are messy birds, and homemade cages are usually harder to keep clean.

A good height for the bird stand is 4 feet. The perch must have a diameter of 2 inches or more. Natural wood perches of larger diameter are better yet. Oak branches make perfect perches for the macaw, both on the stand and in the cage. Perches will have to be replaced periodically.

Building your own aviary setup in the back yard can be done with a very heavy gauge welded wire. You may have to special-order the heavy gauge wire, and it is expensive, but light gauge wire will not hold up well over a long period of time.

The floor of the aviary must be easy to clean and disinfect. Earthen floors are not recommended, for they can become breeding grounds for all sorts of parasites, internal and external. If you must use an earthen floor, cover it with a very thick layer of wood chips. Wood chips can be spot-cleaned and hosed down every day. A thick layer of sand could be used also, but wood chips provide the macaw with plenty of chewing material; sand does not.

The best floor for the outside aviary is poured concrete. The concrete cleans easily and discourages pests from digging their way into the cage. One drawback to concrete is its very hard surface. Concrete floors must be covered with at least 6 inches of wood chips for cushioning. This is imperative for newly acquired birds that may not have full flight.

Outdoor flight cages should be at least 5 feet wide and 6 feet high. The birds should have at least 10 feet of flight space and an extension of 4 feet to 5 feet for a shelter. A well constructed shelter will serve multiple functions. Shelters protect the birds in bad weather. Macaws usually roost in the shelter, and the nest box should be placed there to provide adequate privacy. Nest boxes should never stand out in the rain. The shelter may also be used for a feeding and watering station.

Some people devote a large room to their pet macaw. Design the indoor bird room for easy cleaning. Don't place furniture in the room or the bird will chew it up. Put protective wire on any wooden door frames or window sills. Place more than one stand in the bird room. Put up a few different perches. Design the room for the macaw's safety and comfort. Establish a feeding and watering station. Keep in mind that macaws may chew holes in the plaster before deciding to leave the macaw at liberty in its own room.

Macaws are kept as display birds in zoos, wildlife parks and other attractions. When given a well balanced diet and a naturalistic environment, such as at Parrot Jungle in Miami, Florida, macaws will thrive, reproduce and live to an old age. For many years macaws at Parrot Jungle have been released in the morning and allowed to fly freely throughout the day. In the late afternoon, towards sunset, the birds begin to gather in the treetops close to their roosting area. One or two people with sturdy sticks can then retrieve them as they fly down to the roost.

Training macaws to remain at liberty is a long-term project. The training can be accomplished a few different ways. A feeding and watering station close to or inside the roost must be established and maintained as the birds' main source of feed and water. The birds must be stick-trained before you set them free if you plan to retrieve them nightly and place them in cages. Even if you don't plan to retrieve them nightly, it is wise to have the birds trained to come in when you want them to. Otherwise it would become impossible to check on their health and day-to-day whereabouts. The birds may eventually wander far from familiar ground and get lost.

When two birds show a definite attachment to one another over a period of time, one can be clipped and the other left flighted. The clipped bird should be trained to the stick and to remain sitting on an open stand. The flighted bird should be present during the training lessons inside a flight cage. Once the clipped bird is stick-trained, encourage the flighted bird to sit on the stick next to its mate. Teach it to fly over and land on the stick and on a perch when its mate is there. Once you are confident that the flighted bird will remain close to its clipped mate, take them both out of the flight cage and place them on an open perch together. A cup of fresh water should be available on the perch at all times. After an hour or so, take both birds back to their regular roosting area. Give them their daily ration of feed. Each day the birds should be brought out of the cage and allowed to sit for an hour or so on the same open perch outside the cage. Return them both to the roost and feed them at the same time each day. As the birds become more accustomed to the open perch and their freedom, the period of time can be extended. The pair should always be taken to the same spot to roost at night. The feeding should always be given in the roost as soon as the birds are brought in.

Once the clipped macaw has regained full flight, the routine of going out for the day and in for the night will be well established. The birds may not choose to come in for a couple of nights when the newly flighted bird first regains flight. After a night or two outside they will probably come in, however. Macaws have a very strong roosting instinct. They like to sleep in the same place every night. This instinct, combined with your feeding of the birds as they are returned to the roost in the evening, will eventually establish the birds as reliable free flyers. This is not meant to sound like an easy form of training. It is difficult and time-consuming, and it depends upon consistent effort and rigid routine.

It is not recommended that you try keeping your pet macaw at liberty unless you live out in the country. Residential areas are not appropriate training grounds for free-flying macaws. Even a bird that wants to remain in familiar territory can be chased off by loud noises, dogs or mischievous children. People who have an acre or two of land out in the country can consider training their birds to remain at liberty on their land. Initially the macaw will have to be clipped to familiarize it with the property. Take the clipped bird out to the same tree every day. If possible, trim the tree to keep the parrot within reach of a short pole. Construct a sturdy small shelter and attach it firmly to the tree. Place fresh water in a clean cup near the shelter. Before beginning to take the bird outside and placing it in the tree, do a good job of stick and pole training. The macaw must step onto both the training stick and pole without hesitation or retrieving it will be very difficult. Give the regular feed ration to the bird at the end of the training period on the tree. Immediately retrieve it and bring it into the house.

Never leave the bird unsupervised during the first sessions outside. The first lessons should be kept short. Initially, you just want to get the bird used to the tree as a secure perch. Gradually lengthen the outdoor sessions until you feel confident that the macaw will remain in the tree even if you are not in sight. Walk slowly away from the tree and hide from the bird. Observe its behavior, but don't let the bird see you. The bird will act differently if it can see you watching. Continue training the macaw in this manner and keep a close watch on the growth of new flight feathers on the clipped wing. It may be necessary to re-clip the wing and continue training for close to a year before the macaw can be trusted to remain at liberty and allow itself to be retrieved. Eventually the macaw will remain in the tree on your property even though it has the power of flight. Macaws trained in this way can be a great source of pride for their owners. Usually they can be taught to fly to the owner when called by name. The bird must be rewarded every time it steps onto your arm or flies to it. If you have the time and motivation you can probably train these birds to perform a variety of tricks. (More detailed information on trick training will be given in a later chapter.)

Environments unsuited for macaws are small cages, drafty spots and overly warm rooms. Aviary cages that do not dry out quickly after the rain are not recommended for permanent residences.

EQUIPMENT

As already discussed, macaw cages can be made at home, but the commercially made wrought iron cage is best for indoor living. All macaw cages must be constructed of metal. The bird stand can be bought commercially or can be homemade. No matter what the source, be certain that the base of the stand is stable. The perches for cage and stand should be made of natural wood and replaced periodically. Always make sure that the branches you use have not been sprayed or treated with insecticides or other dangerous chemicals.

Feeders and waterers can be made of very hard plastic or tempered glass. Clay dishes should not be used. The best feed and water dishes are made of stainless steel. Large stainless steel dog dishes, the type sold in pet shops, are perfect for use in the macaw cage or aviary.

A sturdy bird carrier is a necessity for the macaw owner. Again, the pet shop is a good source for a carrier. A heavy-duty hard plastic dog carrier is perfect for macaws. You will need the large size to keep from breaking the bird's long tail. It is not advisable to transport a macaw in an open cage if it is an untame or nervous individual. The sight of so many unfamiliar people and places can stress a bird unnecessarily. Some macaws can be transported in a car (keep the windows rolled up); they enjoy looking out the window at the passing scene. These are well trained, steady birds. But remember, if you are going to the vet, that there are going to be other people in the waiting room with their pet dogs and cats. The carrier may be the better option.

A large bird net is good to have on hand for emergencies or when you have to get the bird out of danger in a hurry. Ask your pet supplier if he can order a macaw net for you. Another possibility is a frame and net used for shrimping. Be sure to use a net with a tight mesh to prevent the parrot from twisting up its toes or damaging the wing bends.

A hospital cage is recommended for people who plan to keep one or more pet birds. Order one from your retail supplier or make one yourself. Use a small cage enclosed on three sides. The front of the cage should open up wide enough to get the bird in and out easily. A perch should be fixed in the box close to the cage bottom. Feed and water dishes should be within easy reach. The bottom must be easy to clean. The hospital cage must have its own heat source and thermostat. You must be able to regulate the temperature and keep it constant for the hospital cage to be effective. The source of heat may be a light bulb or heating strip, but whatever the heat source, be certain that the macaw will not burn itself by coming into contact with it. Disinfect the hospital cage after each use.

Manicure tools should be on hand if you plan to perform the manicure yourself. Buy yourself a small pair of sharp wire cutters or a guillotine style nail clipper made for dogs. If you have never clipped a macaw's claws, have an experienced person show you the procedure before you attempt it yourself. For claws you will want to use a metal nail file to remove sharp edges. For wing clipping, the small wire cutters and a sharp pair of scissors are necessary. Also buy a styptic powder such a Kwik Stop from your local pet retailer.

FEEDING THE MACAW

When you first bring the new bird home, try to find out what it prefers in the way of fruit and vegetables. Ask the seller what the bird has been eating and use this information to help you choose the right feeding program for your macaw. (The following information applies to normal dietary maintenance; special feeding schedules for use during taming and training are given in the applicable sections.)

Every day give the bird a portion of high quality sunflower seed and a few raw peanuts. Other nuts that the bird may enjoy are walnuts, pecans, Brazil nuts, hazel nuts and others. It is not necessary to crack open the nuts for a macaw. Breaking open the shell is good exercise for the macaw, and many birds eat tiny pieces of the shell. Don't overfeed nuts. They are good in moderation. Nuts are high in protein and calorie content.

Small seeds may be accepted readily. Try oats, hemp, millet, chick seeds and dry peas or beans. Always feed the staple seed and experiment with the others to discover what the bird likes the most.

Each day provide the macaw with fruit and vegetable food. A good daily formula is one green and one yellow vegetable and two different fruits. Raw corn, yellow squash, green squash, beans, peas, tomatoes and yams are just some of the vegetables that you may give the macaw. Apples, oranges, mangoes, bananas, pears and peaches, as well as strawberries and a variety of other berries, can be given in daily rations or as treats. Sprinkle all of the soft food with a good brand of mineral powder; powdered supplements are available at pet shops. Just be certain to provide the mineral powder on a daily basis.

Use Linatone by Lambert Kay on the bird's seed every other day. If the macaw is having feather or skin problems, use the Linatone every day. Linatone is an oil-based supplement synthesized for the skin and fur of dogs and cats. The skin and plumage of macaws are conditioned by the ingredients in Linatone. If you wish to mix your own conditioning oil, buy cod liver oil with added vitamins (A and D) and mix it half and half with wheat germ oil. Don't use both the Linatone and other oil at the same time. Give the macaw a piece of romaine lettuce or chicory once in a while.

Every day scrub the water cup and give the bird fresh water with Avitron vitamin supplement added. Avitron is manufactured by Lambert Kay and is manufactured for use with birds.

Newly acquired macaws should be encouraged to eat whatever they like and plenty of it. Get the bird on a good diet first and worry about training it later.

A good maintenance diet for a macaw one year and over follows:

Sunflower seed, oats, hemp: daily.

Two hard dog chew biscuits: daily.

Six to eight raw peanuts: daily.

Other nuts every other day (and as treats).

Two vegetables and two fruits, sprinkled with Vionate: daily.

Other fruits and vegetables as treats.

Fresh water with Avitron vitamin supplement: daily.

A mineral block should be provided for the macaw periodically. See what your bird does with a mineral block. Some macaws chew them to powder as soon as they get new mineral blocks, while others chew them a bit and keep them as toys. There is no need to give mineral blocks on a daily basis if your bird likes to powder them. Use your judgment.

Mineral grit is beneficial to your macaw if given in a clean dish. Soiled gravel or sand is *not* good mineral supplementation for the macaw. Macaws that live in aviaries with earthen floors like to dig up small rocks to chew. These rocks probably provide one source of mineral supplementation. As for grinding the food, mineral grit and rock fragments are not passed through the system easily. They remain in the bird's system and do not have to be replaced daily. Provide a good, clean mineral grit periodically.

You should learn to remain flexible when it comes to feeding a macaw. Feeding requirements may change as a function of environment and physiological changes. A molting macaw may require more feed to maintain its weight than usual. The bird may eat less in the summer than in the winter. Whatever the bird's habits in feeding, a good macaw owner knows what is normal for his parrot and is sensitive to its changing requirements.

Breeding macaws and very young babies should be given the regular maintenance diet and some additional enriched foods. Mix up whole wheat bread with raw egg and milk. Feed this to the bird at room temperature and leave it for a short time before removing it. Always be sure that you have cleaned up any spills of this bread/egg/milk mixture. Old egg and milk can make a macaw very ill.

Also feed green leafy vegetables to breeding birds and young babies on a daily basis. The green food is essential for hens during egg production, and young birds need the calcium for developing bone and muscle tissue.

Very old or sick birds may have to be fed more than once a day. These parrots may have difficulty keeping their weight up if fed only once a day. Be certain to feed these macaws all three of the supplements suggested (a powdered mineral, a water-soluble vitamin and an oil).

Some macaws tend to be fat. These individuals must be given a well balanced low-calorie diet if they are to remain healthy. For these macaws the diet should consist mainly of fruits and vegetables, with seed and nuts added. We tend to feed captive parrots a diet of sunflower seed and peanuts with an occasional piece of fruit. In the wild, macaws probably never eat dried sunflower seed; if they get it at all it is probably in the "milk" stage. A macaw in a banana tree will eat all it can until full. When you have a bird that shows definite signs of overweight (especially if the bird is clipped and inactive), go ahead and slowly alter the diet to include more soft foods, fruits and vegetables than hard seed and nuts.

Macaws with feather problems should be fed an enriched diet as described for ailing birds. Make sure to give all of the suggested supplements. In addition, give the bird a great deal of chewing material. Chewing material will help distract the bird from destroying its feathers. Give fresh branches that you are certain have not been sprayed with insecticides or fertilizers. Give scrap lumber cut into six-inch lengths. A six-inch length of 2 x 4 every day will occupy the macaw and take its mind off feather chewing. Sometimes feather chewing is caused by an insufficient diet, lack of attention or an acquired bad habit. If the diet does not satisfy the bird's needs, change it to the diet described in this chapter. If the bird is not getting at least two hours of your attention (handling) each day, structure yourself to give it more time or consider selling the macaw to someone who has time. An acquired vice is difficult to break, so don't be fooled into buying a feather-plucker for a premium price. Be aware that the condition may never change, but if you still want the bird go ahead and buy it.

Collaring a macaw to keep it from chewing its feathers is a bad idea. The collar will annoy the bird and probably not last through the day. The bird will roll, claw and shake until the collar is off. Some people suggest submitting the parrot to total darkness to interrupt the chewing habit. This may or may not work. If you do see improvement after subjecting the bird to darkness, understand that the darkness will also interfere with its desire to eat normally. Darkness makes the bird sleep almost constantly and may or may not work. Just be certain that the bird does not lose too much weight.

Never spray chemicals onto the macaw to discourage chewing. If you must, use only the commercially marketed preparations to discourage feather chewing. Don't endanger your bird by using the home remedies of a well-meaning friend.

GENERAL CARE OF THE MACAW
AND ITS ACCESSORIES

Daily maintenance includes a routine cleaning of the cage and bird stand. Throw away paper or wood chips on the cage bottom and replace with fresh material. Clean out the feed dish and replace with fresh feed. Wash the feed dishes every couple of days or every day if necessary. The water dish must be scrubbed with hot water, soap and a sponge or brush *every* day. Rinse thoroughly and refill with vitamin water.

Use the cleaning time to check on the bird's droppings, for they are the best indications of good or poor health. One loose dropping is no problem, but a whole day's worth of loose, watery stools should get your attention. Bad stools and leftover feed are a good reason to see the vet without delay. If you find that the macaw is eating less and less feed, keep a close watch on its weight. At different times of the year the bird may require different amounts of feed. If the bird is eating less but still has good weight, don't worry; just adjust the diet, offer the bird as much as it wants and be certain to give supplements.

Periodically sponge off the bars of the cage with plain warm water. Scrub and disinfect the cage bottom and grill. Rinse and dry completely before replacing under the macaw.

Clean the perches on the stand and in the bird cage to keep them free of food and fecal residues. Use a piece of sand paper or a perch scraper. Replace the perches when they become worn down or chewed up. If you wash the perches, let them dry completely before putting the macaw in its cage to roost or on the stand for the day. Standing on wet perches can dispose the macaw to a variety of illnesses. Wash off bird toys if they become soiled.

Bathe the macaw often, every day in warm weather if you want. Macaws love to bathe. Always give the bath in the morning and in sunny weather to allow the bird plenty of time to dry before sundown. Use a spray bottle if you want to mist the parrot. In an outdoor aviary, offer the macaw a large dish of water. The dish must be heavy enough to remain in one place as the macaw jumps into and out of the water. Use plain water for the macaw's bath. Feather shine sprays are not necessary. If the macaw has been given a proper diet, the feathers should have a natural sheen.

Daily maintenance of your pet macaw requires that you change the seed and clean the seed dish every day.

Do NOT clip a macaw's wings like this! The outer primary feather should not be cut (for cosmetic reasons), and each feather should be examined from underneath before it is cut to be sure that blood feathers are not severed.

Clipping the Claws and the Wing

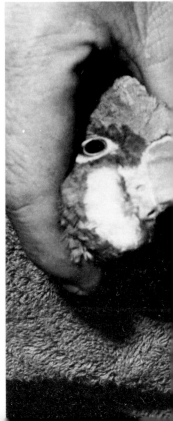

All parrots must have their claws trimmed periodically. This can be done with a small wire cutters as shown here or with a nail file. In any case, it is best to file the claw after it has been cut to remove sharp edges.

The macaw must have its claws manicured periodically. To clip the claws properly you will need a good pair of small wire cutters, a metal nail file or emery board and styptic powder. Styptic pencils are too hard to clot the blood; use the powder. Always work in good light or you risk unnecessary accidents.

Two people must work together to clip the claws. One is responsible for holding the bird while the other clips the claws. To grab an unwilling macaw takes some practice, so if you have never done it, have an experienced person show you how it's done. It is not recommended that you use gloves to grab a macaw. The pressure bite of a macaw is as harmful as the cutting bite. Gloves will not protect you from pressure bites, and they will frighten the bird more than necessary.

One possible method for grabbing an untamed or unpettable bird is to place it on the floor and throw a large towel over its head and torso. Grab the macaw around the back of the neck, with the thumb beneath the lower mandible, being careful not to squeeze or twist the neck. Use your other hand to hold the bird's torso down until your assistant gets hold of the bird's feet and turns it over on its back. The holder must sit on a chair with the bird on his lap.

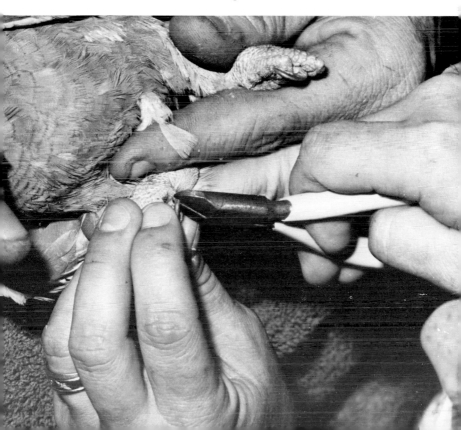

When the two of you are holding onto the bird and moving to a chair, be careful to coordinate your movements to protect the parrot. Don't pull on the legs, neck or body. When you, the holder, are sitting with the bird's head under control in one hand, have the other person hand you the feet. Place two fingers between the bird's legs and hold in the wings with your thumb and pinky.

Let the person clipping take one toe after another and tip the claw. Tipping means just that. Take only the *tip* off the claw. You can always take off more, but you can't put it back. Take off about an eighth of an inch, and no more than a quarter of an inch, in any one clipping. For badly overgrown claws, you may have to repeat the clipping at two-week intervals to get the claws down to a normal length. Don't take too much at one clipping or you will hit blood.

First tip all eight claws and then file each one to remove sharp edges. Work as quickly as you can, but be careful not to clip the claws too short. If you begin filing a nail and hit blood, stop filing, treat with styptic powder and go on to file the others.

If you hit blood, take the styptic powder and press it into the end of the claw. Wait a minute and see if the bleeding stops. Very heavy bleeding may require that you press on the styptic powder with a dry cotton ball. When bleeding is heavy and hard to stop, quickly finish up and possibly stop without finishing. The longer you hold the bird, the faster its heart will beat and the more the bleeding that will occur. Place the macaw back in its cage and cover the bottom with clean paper to keep watch on the amount of bleeding. A drop of blood every couple of minutes will soon coagulate and stop. A quick flow should be observed for no more than five minutes before action is taken. Don't grab the bird up in a panic. If bleeding slows, wait another five minutes before grabbing the bird a second time. If you do feel it necessary to grab the bird again, hold it and medicate with styptic powder until the bleeding stops. Place the bird back into its cage carefully to keep from reopening the bleeding nail tip. Don't bother the bird by constantly looking at it. Let it rest in a quiet cage. Leave the macaw in its cage for a day or two before handling it again, to let the end of the vein heal.

When you are finished with a nail clipping and have not hit blood, place the bird back down on the floor and let it go. First let go of the feet and then the head. Never let the bird go in mid-air. Always think about what you are doing and place the bird down on the floor when you are finished.

You can then retrieve the bird with a stick or your arm and place it back onto the stand or play with it. Make up by offering a peanut.

Other methods for grabbing up the macaw also require practice. You can pin a macaw beneath the lower mandible with a training stick. Be very careful not to injure the bird. Once the macaw is pinned on the ground (but never on a hard surface), use your foot to hold down the stick while you grab the bird around the head with your thumb under the lower mandible and your other fingers surrounding the head and neck. Then grab the feet, using two fingers between the legs. Let the pressure off the pinning stick and lift the macaw. This method requires a great deal of know-how and practice. Don't try this method if you don't know what you are doing, for you could break the bird's neck or injure it severely by pressing too hard on the neck.

A net may be handy for catching very wild birds. Drop the net over the bird's head and grab it behind the head (around the neck) right through the net. Have a second person help you untangle the bird's claws and hold the feet. Then take your free hand, slip it into the net and grab the bird around the head and neck. Once you have a good hold on the bird's neck, let go with the hand outside the net. Take the feet from the second person and sit down with the bird on your lap.

Regardless of how you catch the bird, always have all of your equipment gathered before beginning. When you are finished with the manicure, always place the parrot back down on the floor before letting go of it.

Now that you have learned to grab the macaw and hold it without injuring it, you may want to clip the feathers of *one* wing to restrict flight. With the holder doing his job, take one hand and extend the wing at the wing bend. Hold it securely, but don't bend it out from the body at a bad angle. Look at both wings. If there are blood feathers (new feathers that are still growing in) on one wing and not the other, clip the one that doesn't have blood feathers on it and be certain that the new feathers are protected from breakage. If there are no blood feathers present on either wing, leave the better-feathered wing alone and clip the other.

In addition to the small wire cutters and styptic powder that you used to clip the claws, you will need a sharp pair of scissors and good light.

Extend the wing and leave the outer primary flight feather as it is. Do not clip the outer primary or you subject the bird to unnecessary risk of injury. Clip the second and third feathers in half with the scissors. Clip off the next seven or eight feathers with the wire cutters. Do *not* clip these particular feathers with scissors. Use wire cutters for a straight cut across the quill. Clip off the feathers at the point at which the feather begins to emerge from the quill. If the feathers fluff out too close to the edge of the wing (within two inches), don't cut them off at that point. Always leave at least two to three inches of feather shaft emerging from the edge of the wing to cushion it from injury.

Macaws are heavy birds, so there is no need to clip both wings to restrict flight. Of course there is variation in size and strength from bird to bird. It is important for you to be aware of your bird's flying behavior and take it into account when you clip the wing. Very sedate birds should not be clipped as heavily as flighty birds. Small strong birds may require having one or two more feathers clipped off to keep them from flying.

Be absolutely certain that you can identify the blood feathers (if there are any present) before you begin clipping the wing. If there is any doubt in your mind, do not attempt the procedure. You could cause the bird considerable damage and possible death if you clip off a blood feather.

Whenever you decide to clip a wing that has blood feathers on it, do not clip away the feathers on either side. If you do, the blood feather has no protection from breakage and may be damaged by mistake when you are handling the parrot. Learn to TIP the blood feather, and leave feathers of the same length on either side to protect it.

After completing the clip job, place the macaw down on the floor and release first the feet and then the head. Never release the macaw in mid air. Retrieve the bird with a training stick or your hand and place it onto the bird stand or back into its cage to let it settle down.

Pulling feathers instead of clipping them is not a good choice. Whenever a feather is plucked a new feather begins to grow immediately from the feather follicle. When a bird has to replace a number of feathers at once, the bird becomes stressed. Food requirements are greater, and the bird's entire system becomes disposed toward growing new feathers. The bird's resistance to disease may be weakened if it has to undergo rapid, abundant feather growth. Clipping the feathers of the wing is a better choice.

The clipped feathers fall out and are replaced in approximately five or six months. Feather growth and replacement occur at different rates in different individuals. Whenever you are in the habit of taking your bird out in the yard or out to an unfamiliar place for the day, keep a close watch on the progress of feather replacement. The macaw may not have flown for many months, but when it suddenly discovers its new ability, it may be excited enough to take off. A bird that is not a practiced flyer may want to return to you but be unable to control the direction of its flight.

The holder is responsible for holding the macaw still without harming it. The holder must glance at the bird's eyes occasionally to watch for signs of excessive stress. Whenever the eyes stop dilating as a response to changing light, the bird is undergoing severe stress. The holder must be careful not to restrict the macaw's free breathing. At the same time, the holder has a responsibility to the person working with him. It is important not to let the bird get a bite hold on the person that is clipping. If at any time the holder has to let go of the bird or he feels that the macaw may break free, he owes a fair warning to the person doing the clipping. A simple "Letting go!" is better than no warning at all, but giving a few seconds' notice is best.

Both parties, the clipper and the holder, should know what they are going to do and have all of the necessary equipment before beginning. Work quickly and carefully.

Never learn to perform these procedures by doing them. You should always learn to clip the claws and feathers by having an experienced person show you how it is done. Otherwise you are asking for a disaster. Three individuals can suffer injury: the macaw and both people involved.

Clipping the wing should be a prelude to taming of the macaw. There is no reason to clip the wing and leave the bird sitting in its cage.

Grabbing up and holding the macaw still without harming it is a skill that is developed by practice. Experienced bird handlers are just as careful when releasing the bird as they are when they grab it and hold it.

You should never just let go your grip on a macaw and let it fall to the floor. If you are holding the macaw with the feet in one hand and the head in the other you will be either sitting down with the bird resting on its back in your lap or you will be standing with the bird held against a PADDED work counter. The counter top must be clear of all other objects.

Lift the macaw off your lap or counter and hold it so that the feet are touching the ground. The bird is no longer on its back. Let go of the feet and legs first, then let go of the head. Retrieve the bird from the floor with a stick or your hand (if the bird is tame).

If you have just clipped a new bird and are planning to begin taming, be certain to clip the wing and release the bird in a safe taming area. Your first task is to train the bird to a training stick to make it safely transportable from training area to cage.

When releasing the macaw into a hospital cage after treating it for an injury, you will want to be very careful. If the macaw can be placed into the cage with its feet on the perch and released without falling to the cage bottom, fine. Most of the time you can place the macaw on the bottom of the cage and release it. Release the feet first and then the head.

If you have captured the bird in a towel and held it wrapped up that way, put it on the bottom of the cage or on the floor and release the bird. Let it climb out of the towel.

Macaws are individuals with individual personalities. Some are clowns, constantly "showing off," while others are quiet and docile . . . just like people!

Personality

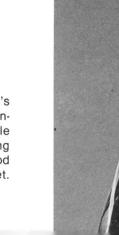

You can often look into a bird's face and tell whether it is an untamable bronco or a gentle creature. This watermelon-eating macaw appears to be a good candidate for a pet.

Macaws are extremely intelligent birds with a complex emotional makeup. They have emotions much the same as those of children. They are very self-centered creatures, always seeking attention. Their desire for attention is the main reason that macaws are so trainable. Attention-getting behavior can take many forms and be a real problem if the macaw owner does not know how to deal with it properly.

Macaws can also develop jealous behavior. They can become jealous of their human owners or their feathered companions. Some macaws are easily frightened, while others are not bothered by anything. Some are nervous, others sedate.

Macaws have memory and are capable of problem-solving. They actually think. Memory and cognitive ability vary from individual to individual. Very young birds can be taught to use their minds for solving problems, just as children are. Birds learn how to learn. Young birds can learn both expressive and comprehensive language. Expressive language means that the macaw can verbalize. Comprehensive language means that the bird can learn to associate certain spoken words with activities. Both young and older macaws can develop expressive language, although older birds usually take longer to acquire speech.

Hand-reared macaws can be affectionate or aggressive. Hand-rearing does not change the personality of the macaw, but it does make the bird tame to people. Some hand-feds I have known were spoiled, nippy birds. Not all hand-fed macaws enjoy being petted. The great majority of hand-feds can make superb pets if trained properly. The same can be said for wild-caught or parent-reared young.

Most macaws that are wild when you first get them settle down in a few weeks and adjust to a new routine. Daily routine helps give the bird security. You may encounter a macaw that is extremely nervous. Such a bird may have difficulty adjusting to its new environment. For these individuals, strict adherence to a feeding, cleaning and taming routine is recommended. The rigid routine will help the nervous macaw. It will know what to expect from you in a short time. The macaw's actions and responses will begin to make more sense to you as they become more predictable.

The average macaw is a steady individual that adjusts rapidly to changes in its environment. It is mischievous, playful and somewhat destructive. The average bird reacts positively to your attempts at taming.

Some imported or tube-fed baby macaws may be frantic. Whenever a person approaches, the bird begins to scream and back away into the corner of its cage. These frantic birds are usually tamable, but they take much more time and patience than most.

Aggressive macaws must be approached cautiously (so must frantic birds) to avoid getting bitten. This is not to suggest that you will not get bitten when taming an aggressive macaw. With practice, an experienced parrot trainer can minimize the risk of being bitten while taming the bird. Those who undertake the taming of a large parrot like a macaw should understand the hazards of the task. It is like being a construction worker or a mechanic; there are built-in dangers to the job. There is very little you can do to protect yourself from the pressure bite of an angry macaw. Gloves do not prevent your hand from being squeezed.

Macaw bites can be grouped into two types, the pressure bite and the bite that breaks the skin. Pressure bites result in bruises and swellings. Bites that break the skin should be treated like any other puncture wound. Some are superficial, but others result in deep wounds. Macaws do not transmit rabies through their bite.

You may buy a macaw from a private individual who had the bird for a few years. These birds may be tame to one person and vicious to others. These are difficult birds to deal with unless a strict behavior modification program is instituted to change the undesirable behavior, most often biting.

They may be moody birds that one minute ask to be petted and the next moment whip around to bite you. Again, a behavior modification program must be used to effectively change the bad behavior.

Bronco is a name given to parrots that refuse to tame down. True broncos resist all your efforts to tame them. They continue to bite even though you have adhered completely to your structured behavior program. Broncos do exist, but not in large numbers. People who tame many parrots do not often report encountering broncos (unless they use the term erroneously). If, after many months of dedicated work, you cannot make any change in the macaw's behavior, you can try a few alternatives. Find a very experienced person to do the taming for you or teach you how to do it. This is not always easy. Possibly the experienced person may agree that the bird is untamable. If this is the case, you may try selling the bird to a breeder of macaws. Breeding birds are often fierce individuals. The hobbyist or professional bird breeder is not concerned with how well the bird relates to people—just how well it relates to other macaws. Your retail pet shop or local zoo may be able to put you in contact with a breeder of macaws. Under no circumstances should you attempt to sell this macaw to other people without telling them the truth about the bird.

Some macaws are emotionally imbalanced. These birds are very difficult to deal with and usually take a long time to tame. Some of the bad behaviors that they develop cannot be tolerated in a family setting. As with the bronco, you should make an effort to find these birds a suitable home with a breeder or fancier who is willing to accept the bird as it is if it cannot be made into a pet.

The average macaw is a steady individual that adjusts rapidly to changes in its environment providing its basic needs of feed and security are met.

Handfeeding peanuts can be a useful procedure in taming, but shy strangers who might shriek and pull their hands away when the bird approaches to take the peanut may cause more harm than good.

Taming the Macaw

A tame macaw is one that will sit on your shoulder and feel secure enough to eat. Feeding your macaw dog biscuits is acceptable, but they should not be a major part of a macaw's diet.

Taming a macaw is not the same as training it. A tame macaw should have a few basic behaviors, including stepping onto your arm or the arm of others without biting. A macaw that does not step onto your arm without biting is not a tame bird and should not be represented as one. The tame macaw will remain sitting on a bird stand or on your arm for at least a few minutes at a time without attempting to jump off. Tame birds may or may not enjoy having their heads or bodies touched, but most do.

Training a macaw begins with the most basic behavior, remaining on the stand for an extended period of time without direct supervision (stick training is recommended), and ends with the bird mastering a variety of complicated behaviors including speech and tricks.

Before you begin your first lesson with the wild macaw, you must set aside a suitable taming area. This must be a room without a lot of furniture for the bird to crash into. The floor must be carpeted or padded for the bird's safety. Breakable objects must be removed from the room, for the macaw is likely to have everything thrown over in the first few lessons.

Equip the taming area with a sturdy bird stand; the plain "T" style is best for taming. Get yourself two 3-foot-long training sticks and one short training stick. Their diameter should be 1½-2".

Do not use a net to retrieve a macaw during the taming lesson. Nets are not going to help the bird gain trust in you and should be used only when you have to catch the bird in an emergency. It is not recommended that you wear gloves when taming a macaw. Gloves make the bird regard you the same as it regarded its captors, and they do not protect you very much from the bite of a macaw. It is better to be careful and concentrate on what you are doing to avoid getting bitten more than necessary. If you must use gloves, wear the tight-fitting leather kind that is available in sporting goods stores. Gloves should always be a neutral shade or skin tone.

Most bites are not very dangerous anyway. They hurt but they soon go away. Consider this: when the macaw bites you it is usually just as bad an experience for the bird as it is for you. Most people react dramatically when the bird bites them, which scares the bird even more. It is fine to react to the bird's bite as long as you are consistent with your reaction.

When you get the bird home it may already be clipped. If not, you should clip one wing before beginning to tame the macaw. Read the description of wing clipping completely before attempting to do it.

If the macaw is really shaken up by its new surroundings, let it settle down for a little while before beginning the first lesson. Be prepared to spend a long time in the first lesson, at least one hour, maybe more. Getting the bird out of its cage is the first problem. If possible, move the cage into the taming area and let the bird out in there. If you try to move it from one room to another you may run into lots of trouble.

When the bird comes out of the cage, let it look around a minute. Then present the long stick to the macaw and coax it to step on. Some step right on and can be taught to step off and on the stick in just a few minutes. If this is the case with the bird that you are taming, be assured that you have chosen a good candidate.

Some macaws refuse to come out of the cage. Be patient. It may help to stay away from in front of the door. Get behind the cage and see if the bird will go away from you and out the door. You may have to close the door behind the bird or it will climb back into the cage. Sometimes you may have to leave the taming area for a minute to get the bird to come out. Most come out with you in the room in a short time. Others pop out as soon as the cage door is open. Birds that are scared to come out soon learn to enjoy time outside the cage.

Once the bird is out in the taming area, get the cage out of your work space. Stick training is the first thing that the macaw must learn. As soon as the bird is trained to remain on a stick, you will be able to leave the cage in a permanent location and move the bird around on a stick. To accomplish stick training, offer the stick to the macaw horizontally to its body and in front of the feet. Work with the bird from the padded floor. Keep the bird low to the floor until it is steady on the stick. Let it step on, then keep it there a moment and place it back down on the floor. Repeat the procedure until the macaw steps onto the stick readily whenever you present it.

Some birds are difficult to stick-train. You may spend your first hour or two with the new bird just trying to get it to perch on a training stick. Don't give up trying to stick-train the macaw or you won't get any further in your attempts at taming. Present the stick to the bird in front of both its feet. Touch the bird gently with the stick against both legs. If it won't step up, press the stick against the legs for an instant and release the pressure. Try this a few times. If the bird still doesn't step on, try touching the bird's toes with the stick lightly for a few seconds. Very stubborn macaws may need to have the stick pushed against their bodies in an upward motion. Try to get these birds to at least step over the stick. Once you get the feet moving, the stick will find its way into the bird's grip. Go on from there. If necessary, spend all of the time in your first lesson on training the macaw to step onto the stick and remain there.

Once the bird steps onto the stick, lift it off the floor and walk slowly around. Don't leave the taming area. Walk and stop for a minute. Talk to the macaw. Walk, stop, talk. After a few minutes place the macaw on the stand and let it sit for a minute. Then begin again. As you move around the room with the macaw on a stick, try to keep the bird facing you. Learn to use your body to block escape attempts. With the bird facing away from you it will be tempted to jump.

If the bird jumps, don't run after it excitedly. Slowly move toward the parrot; offer the stick and begin again. Drilling the macaw to step onto the stick from the floor and from the stand, to step off the stick onto the floor and the stand and to walk around with you while sitting on the stick is one of the most important parts of taming.

Part of stick training involves leaving the taming area and walking slowly from room to room with the bird. The first trip outside the taming area should be to an adjoining room. Walk in, then stop and stand still for a moment; talk to the bird. Then slowly walk back to the taming area. Continue with this advanced stick training until you can walk all over the house with the macaw. Whenever it jumps from the stick, retrieve it and continue the lesson.

Work the macaw from the T-stand to arm train it. Once the bird has learned to step unhesitatingly onto the stick, you are ready to begin arm training. Don't try to train the macaw to your hand. It is far too large to be comfortable on your hand. Offer your arm to the bird horizontally to its body and in front of the legs. Use your free hand to distract the bird's attention from your extended arm. Hold the free hand to the side and slightly above the bird's eye level.

Some macaws reach for your arm readily and step on. Others put one foot on your arm and leave the other on the perch. With these birds use a constant slow movement of your arm to force the macaw to step up with the other foot. Always use your free hand to distract the bird's attention. If the bird has a firm grip on the perch and refuses to step onto your arm even though you press against its legs, try touching the toes lightly with your free hand. This often makes the bird lift at least one foot and place it on your arm. With one foot on your arm and the other holding firmly to the stand, again touch the toes lightly and see if you can maneuver the bird's foot onto your arm. Rest your arm against the bird stand perch if necessary. Your primary goal is to get the bird's feet onto your arm.

Keep in mind that the great majority of parrots, small and large alike, use their beaks to test any prospective perch, even if they have stepped onto it a hundred times. Many novice trainers mistake this testing action for an attempted bite and pull their arms out of the bird's reach. This reaction to the bird's pressing its beak against your arm is going to have bad results. The bird will begin to distrust the arm as a safe perch. It is not suggested that you allow the macaw to bite you and offer no reaction. Use a loud "NO" if the bird attempts to bite you. You must learn to become strategic with the use of the word "NO." If timed properly, the negative word may be enough to stop the bird from biting. At the same time, move your distracting hand to draw the bird's attention. Most macaws do not grab onto your arm and refuse to let go. The majority will give you a pinch or a quick pressure bite and then withdraw.

For macaws that continually try to bite when you offer them your arm, try coaxing them with food. To be effective you will have to institute a feeding schedule that gives the bird a limited amount of time to eat its daily ration of feed and vegetables. Instead of feeding the bird in the morning and leaving food in the cage all day, feed the bird in the late afternoon or evening, after you have finished training for the day. Give the bird two hours to eat its fill and then remove the feed. (But remember that fresh water should *always* be available to the bird.) Do not begin feeding in the afternoon and evening until you are certain that your new macaw is eating well and maintaining its weight. New birds may be off their feed for a couple of days until they get used to the new environment. It is imperative that the new macaw get off to a good start in your home. Wait for at least one week before changing the feeding time. Wait longer with macaws that make the adjustment slowly. You cannot starve a bird into becoming tame, and you cannot tame a sick bird. Be sure that the bird is eating well; use the changed feeding time only if the bird is stubbornly refusing to step onto your arm.

If the macaw should bite you and not let go, use your free hand to push against the lower mandible. Try to push your arm or hand farther into the bird's mouth. This action will make the bird lose control of the situation and let go. Don't try to pry the bird's bill off your skin; you won't be able to. Don't strike the macaw unless it absolutely refuses to let go.

Birds that bite every time the arm is presented must be handled differently. Use the training stick to drill the bird in stepping up from the stand; pass the bird under the stand and make it step back onto the stand. Keep drilling the bird until it begins to get tired. The bird will pant when it is tired and overheated. Once you feel that it is very tired, try offering your arm. Have your free hand ready and if necessary tap the bird lightly to prevent it from making contact. Now to "tap lightly" does *not* mean to hit the parrot. If you pay attention to what you are doing and use the verbal "NO" and your free hand to touch the bird's bill when it goes at you (before it gets you), the macaw will become tame to the arm without having to be hit. Use the stick to drill the bird over and over if it tries to bite every time you offer your arm. This is the appropriate time for the marathon session. Spend as much time as it takes to break the bird of biting. Tire it out to the point that it will step wherever you want it as long as the lesson gets done.

There is a distinct difference between taming and breaking a macaw. Taming implies that the parrot develops the desired behavior (stepping onto the arm without biting) without a lot of heavy handling.

When a macaw needs breaking, you must employ some strong-arm techniques. With these difficult macaws it is recommended that you find an experienced trainer to assist in the taming process. It is unwise for the novice trainer to expect to strong-arm a very tough individual without both parties getting hurt. Far better to find a person who has handled other tough birds. These trainers can accomplish the task of breaking without harming the bird and at the same time without suffering too many severe bites.

With some very tough macaws it may take many months to make a positive change in behavior. These changes will happen over a period of time as long as you, the trainer, persist in the daily lessons, use a feeding schedule and stick to the routine. If the macaw takes six or seven months to tame down but the task is accomplished in the end, what does it matter that it took so long? You will probably have the bird for many, many years—so devoting a few months to taming it should not be too much to expect.

Most macaws will not take months to tame, however, so don't let a single tough bird ruin your attitude toward macaws as pets. Macaws take special handling from the very first day to the very last that they are in your care. They are everything that a small parrot is, greatly magnified. They make more noise, they bite harder, they eat a more varied diet and require more space to live in.

Taming a large parrot should never be taken lightly. It is an involved task for bird and trainer alike. Each macaw is an individual, and most react differently to the same taming techniques. Do not read this material and expect it to work in every case with every macaw. Be versatile enough to adjust the suggested techniques to meet your needs with each bird.

When the macaw steps onto your arm for the first time, keep it there for as long as you can. Talk softly to the parrot, using its name. Repeat the name in a soft tone of voice. Some birds calm down to a soft singing voice. After the macaw has remained on your arm for at least five minutes without jumping, place it back onto the stand and begin again.

Arm taming should be done in the same manner as stick training. Drill the bird over and over in stepping from the stand to your arm and back to the stand. Always let the bird remain sitting on your arm for a few minutes if it desires. If the macaw likes to sit you are way ahead of the game.

Offer the macaw a raw peanut or a small bit of raw corn as a reward for correct behavior. The bird may drop the reward as soon as it is in its beak, but offer it anyway. Taming and training can be a little messy if you use soft food for rewards. Try to get the macaw to take sunflower seed and peanut bits instead.

With the macaw perched comfortably on your arm, slowly move your arm away from the stand and close to your body. If the bird jumps back to the stand, begin again. Continue until you have the bird sitting still on your arm. Keep your elbow bent at a normal angle to keep the macaw from climbing to your shoulder. That will come later. First it is imperative that your bird learn to perch on your arm and remain there.

Petting the macaw may come very easily in your taming or it may take a long time. With some birds petting comes before arm taming. Use your instincts to tell you when touching the bird is appropriate. You may find in the first few lessons that the bird will allow you to touch its feet and abdomen but no other part of the body. Others prefer that you pet their heads and necks. Macaws even enjoy being scratched beneath the wings and on the throat. You may have a macaw that does not want to be touched at all. Take more time with such a bird. Do not use gloves to hold onto the bird and force it to accept petting. This is the worst way to approach pet taming and should never be done.

SPECIAL BEHAVIOR PROBLEMS

Macaws are prone to developing special behavior problems in a household setting. This is because they are extremely intelligent and emotionally complex creatures that usually are too restricted in captivity to keep from getting bored. Given a large flight cage and plenty of activity, a macaw is less likely to develop behavior problems.

The three most prevalent special problems that occur are excessive screaming, extreme jealousy of one or two family members (resulting in biting) and destruction of family property.

Screaming is very difficult to cope with. Macaws are noisy birds and in a residential area may be a disturbance to the peace. Most macaws scream for attention, but others scream for the sheer pleasure of it. When screaming is enjoyed by the bird it becomes its own reinforcement, and there is virtually nothing you can do to train it out of the bird. For macaws that scream for attention there is a basis for dealing with the behavior. You must learn to pay attention to the bird for something other than screaming.

Most macaw owners inadvertently reinforce their bird's screaming by attending to them when they are noisest, when the screaming bothers them the most (for example in the morning when the sun has just come up and in the late afternoon when they have just come home from work). To make the bird quiet, most owners will give it any toy it desires, let it out of the cage unsupervised or feed it. All of these responses to screaming may stop it for the moment, but they are in effect going to *increase* the incidence of the screaming behavior. By giving the macaw what it wants to get quiet, you reinforce the screaming.

Be certain to attend to the bird for NOT screaming. Do not scold the bird when it screams—just mechanically give the bird an unpleasant consequence for its behavior. Cover the cage for three to five minutes (use a dark cover). Uncover the macaw as soon as it is quiet for a minute or two and pay attention to it for *not* screaming. Reward the bird or take it out. If the bird sits out on a stand and screams, place it into the cage until it is quiet. Then take it back out.

Some birds scream because they are wild and want to chase you away. If you leave a wild screamer alone to make it quiet you are reinforcing the screaming. You may have to spend time standing in front of the bird. Wait until it becomes quiet and stays quiet for a couple of minutes before you walk away.

You must be able to understand why the bird is screaming and decide upon an appropriate consequence of undesirable behavior. At the same time, try to substitute a behavior that you can attend to. This will help extinguish undesirable behavior by giving the macaw a better alternative for getting attention.

Biting should be treated in a similar manner. First you should decide why the bird is biting. Is it jealousy? If so, try to remedy this by having the victim of biting make friends with the macaw, with the preferred person absent. If the victim is not willing to deal with the parrot on an individual basis, there is no way to change the bird's behavior. Better to keep the object of its aggressions away. If the victim is willing to deal with the jealous macaw, try the following suggestions.

Try to make friends with the bird first with food. Spend time talking to the bird and feeding it goodies. Try to give the bird a more enjoyable way to relate to you. Play with it. Get a chain and play tug. Use your imagination. Try to substitute an acceptable behavior for an unacceptable one.

You may be able to modify biting behavior by giving the bird a daily speech lesson. This enables you to reinforce the parrot for a very desirable behavior. It also helps the macaw develop its personality potential. To be sure, macaws will undergo personality development. It is up to you to help the bird develop a good personality. If you don't, there may come a time when the macaw will be too much for you to deal with in a household setting.

You may have to spend over a year to modify biting behavior in a macaw that lived in another household for many years. Most macaws respond well to strict behavior modification programming. If you put in the time, you will get favorable results.

Macaws are chewers. Some chew more than others. It should become part of your routine to provide the macaw with plenty of chewable material. If you do not, the macaw may chew up some of your personal possessions. The wooden furniture will bear the bird's distinctive mark. Wall paneling, leather shoes and purses, picture frames, pictures, curtains, clothing, books and everything else in the house are possible chew toys in the mind of an active macaw. You must channel the bird's chewing activity toward certain objects that you can replace periodically. Give the bird chew toys. Provide chunks of wood for the bird to chew up. Use 5-inch or 6-inch lengths of 2x4 or other lumber; the lumber must be chemically untreated, of course. The macaw will usually splinter the lumber in a very short time. Supply a fresh piece as needed. In addition, give fresh branches complete with leaves, flowers and berries. Always be sure the fresh chewing material is free of insecticides, fertilizers and other harmful agents. Do not leave the macaw to find its own chew toys.

Other special problems may crop up. Try to analyze the bird's behavior in relation to its environment. How do you cope with its behavior? Could you be reinforcing the bird without knowing it? Be as objective as possible, then decide upon a behavior program and stick to it.

THE BEST TRAINER FOR THE MACAW

The best trainer for the wild macaw is a calm person. The sex of the trainer is not as important as the trainer's attitude toward the task of taming a large parrot. A child should never attempt to tame a macaw. Children's smaller hands and limited reach are disadvantages. In addition, a macaw's behavior is not easy for anyone to interpret. Children can develop bad feelings toward birds that have injured them.

The qualities of a good trainer include self-confidence, flexibility and an appreciation of the macaw's complexity. The trainer must not be a quitter or a person who cannot follow through on a long-term project. Sometimes taming the macaw may take a long time. You may have to suspend other activities for over a month. If this is not possible, leave the taming to someone else. Nervous or easily angered individuals may overreact and injure a wild macaw if it should bite them severely, so they should not attempt taming.

If you want to own a pet macaw but do not feel that you can accomplish the task of taming, make certain that there is someone available to tame the bird before you condemn it to a life in a cage.

ONCE THE MACAW IS TAME

After you have taught the bird the basis of tame behavior, you will probably want to take the bird out of the house with you. The best way to begin is by taking the clipped macaw out into your own backyard for short periods of time. Take the bird out on your arm. Bring out the bird stand and work the bird from it on stick and arm. It is important for the macaw to have a secure perch outside.

Keep the bird away from trees. Although it cannot fly, it can climb up into a tree and refuse to come down. If your parrot is good on a short stick, try retrieving it with a long pole if it gets stuck up a tree. You may

The author with her charges at Parrot Jungle in Miami. When she holds a peanut in her hand, the macaws actually "beg" for it.

Macaws can shell peanuts with great skill and dexterity, but they often appreciate shelled peanuts as a special treat.

have to climb up after it and retrieve it on a stick. Don't climb down with the bird; instead hand the macaw down to a person on the ground.

Once the macaw learns to remain on the bird stand outside for a long period of time you may consider taking it to a friend's house for the day. Take the bird stand with you so that the macaw can be comfortable. It is not advisable to take the macaw to a park; strange dogs may frighten it, and strange people may be bitten if they try to touch the bird. If you take the bird to the park on a very quiet weekday, be certain to take the stand and fresh water for the bird. Always be careful when you have your macaw out in public.

Some people like to take their macaws for a ride on a bicycle. This is not fair for a bird that has had its wings clipped. If the bike should go down, the bird will certainly fall to the ground.

If possible, take your bird on vacation with you. Don't leave it sitting in a hotel or motel while you go out and sight-see. Take the parrot only if you plan to spend adequate time with it. Otherwise it is better to leave it at home with a friend or neighbor.

CONCLUSION

When you first get a wild macaw, set up a separate taming area and get the necessary equipment. Clip one wing if necessary. First get the macaw out of the cage in the taming area. Do not try to transport it from a cage to the taming area until it is trained to a stick.

Do stick training first and then perch training. Arm training should be done once the bird has mastered the stick and sits well on the perch. Gloves are not recommended for arm training. Talk to the bird in a soft voice and learn to use a loud "NO" if the macaw goes to bite you. Do not automatically strike the macaw for biting. There are many other ways to deal with biting.

Only one person should work with the macaw in any one session. It is best for one person to do the initial taming, but if a second experienced person wants to deal with the parrot, fine. Just be certain that the taming techniques are the same for both of you.

Offer the bird food rewards even if it doesn't take them. When the macaw steps onto your arm for the first time, let it sit for as long as you can before returning it to the stand.

Give your new bird a taming lesson every day and spend time talking to the parrot when it is in the cage. Be consistent in your reactions to the bird's behavior. Devote plenty of time to the macaw from the first day you get it.

Always feed the bird a good daily ration, even if you find it necessary to change the feeding time.

Children should never attempt the task of taming a large parrot.

Children should never attempt the task of taming any large parrot, for such birds are capable of inflicting painful bites.

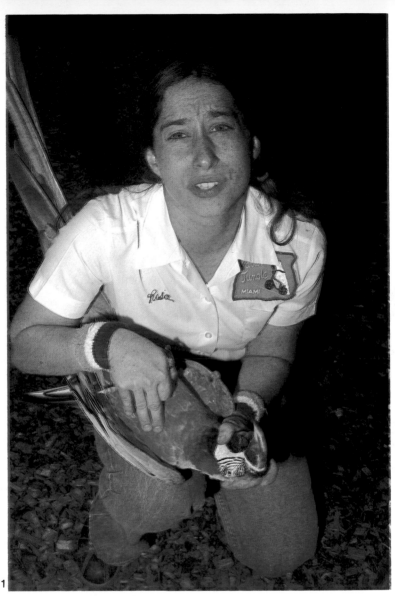

1. The author demonstrating the proper way to hold a macaw when you want to clip its wing, cut its claws or just examine it. Shown during her performance at Parrot Jungle, she implores potential macaw owners to treat their birds with care. 2. To show how intelligent macaws can be, she demonstrates how a macaw can be trained to roll over, again and again, on command. 3. Some macaws can even be taught to "stand" on their shoulders!

2

3

Advanced Training

Not every macaw is trainable, though most are tamable. Older birds, like the macaw shown above which had been caged in a large aviary in a public zoo for 30 years, might be too old to be trained, but young birds, like those shown to the right, are affectionate to each other and might very easily transfer that affection to a human and become intelligently trained pets.

OTHER APPROACHES TO TAMING

In the chapter on taming it is suggested that you be versatile enough to modify the taming methods to achieve the best results. This does not mean that you should try some of the "popular" theories of bird taming, such as wetting the bird, sedating it, keeping it in total darkness or depriving it of food.

I have heard all of these methods and others just as cruel suggested as techniques for taming large parrots. If you have a proper respect for the macaw you will not consider these methods. Wetting the bird and starving it undermine its health. Sedatives should never be used unless the macaw has to undergo surgery. Sedating a bird without harming it is a very difficult thing to do, so the novice bird trainer should not attempt sedation.

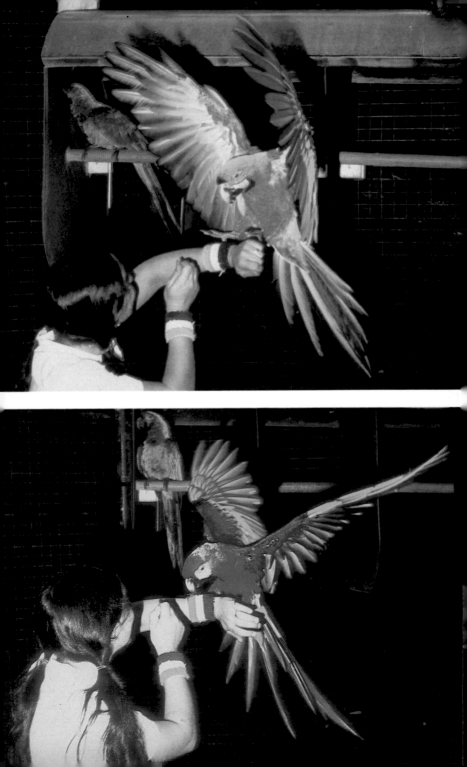

The three photographs on these pages show three different macaw hybrids. The author has trained them to fly onto her arm when she calls them by name. It is very difficult to predict the color of the unborn hybrid.

Light deprivation will cause the macaw to sleep throughout the day and night (a natural reaction to total darkness). Because of its constant roosting state the macaw will not eat a normal amount. Attempting to handle a wild macaw in a poorly lighted room is dangerous for both of you. If you adhere to a behavioral approach you will see positive results in the great majority of cases. With birds that do not seem to respond to behavior modification, you probably are not administering the program properly. Review the section on taming and if possible speak to a behavioral specialist such as a special education teacher or speech therapist.

SPEECH TRAINING

Macaws are very verbal birds. You should teach the bird to say a few words and phrases. You may have an exceptional macaw that will acquire an extensive vocabulary. To teach the macaw to speak you must be able to regiment yourself to give it regular lessons.

Speech lessons are most effective when given many times a day for a few minutes at a time. A 30-minute speech lesson once a day is not as effective as four five-minute lessons. Teach the parrot one word at a time. Most people start with "Hello." Say "Hello" to the bird, slowly and distinctly. Follow the word with the bird's name. Offer a peanut to the bird. In the first lessons it is good to reinforce the desirable behavior of just having the bird paying attention to the lesson. Do not withhold the reward until the macaw comes out with a perfect "Hello." That is unrealistic.

Reward the bird first for attending to the lesson. Later, reward any verbalization at the appropriate time, that is, after you have said the word. When the bird is responding with a verbal sound consistently, begin to reward only for a two-syllable sound, even if the word "Hello" does not resemble the sound. Later, reward for a two-syllable sound that ends in "O." Eventually in this way the bird will learn to repeat the word "Hello" for a reward. After "Hello," go on to other words and short phrases. Macaws are fairly easy to teach because they so crave attention.

Build your macaw's vocabulary the same as you would a child's. First teach simple sounds of one or two syllables and then go onto short three- and four-syllable phrases. Add syllables to lengthen phrases as you teach the bird more and more.

Teach the macaw only one word or phrase at a time. Do not teach only one word of a phrase at a time. Teach the whole phrase together, in one sound.

It is easier to teach a young macaw to speak than an older one. The older macaw will acquire speech if given lessons regularly, but it takes longer. If you have bought an older bird that does not talk, give it lessons and see whether it does not learn. Older birds have been listening to people talk for many years and are already familiar with the sound of speech. They are, however, unfamiliar with talking to people for attention and reinforcement. That is the primary lesson for the older macaw.

The best method for teaching a macaw to speak is to devote your time to the task and speak to it in person. Recorded speech lessons may teach the parrot, but recorded lessons do not hand the bird rewards. There is no need to cover the cage when you give the macaw a speech lesson. It is best to take the bird out of the cage and let it sit on the stand during the lesson. You do not have to dim the lights to get the bird's attention.

The best time of day for giving the speech lesson is when the macaw is at its noisiest. The morning and late afternoon hours are best. If you are home during the day, give a lesson whenever you want. If you work, give the lessons before you leave in the morning (you can leave the macaw in its cage and save time), when you return from work and in the evening.

Unlike the majority of Amazon parrots, macaws have individual voice qualities. Your macaw will learn to speak in its own voice, but your Amazon parrot will sound like you. It may copy the range of your voice, but that is all.

Women make the best speech trainers for macaws and other parrots as well. Men do the job well if they speak slowly and distinctly. With long phrases, you must exaggerate the sounds of vowels and consonants. If you don't the phrase will sound garbled when the bird learns to say it.

When a macaw talks on *command*, this means that the bird repeats what you say after you say it. You should try to teach your macaw command speech, for it is a very good way to develop your bird's personality and helps establish a good rapport between bird and person.

A more specialized form of speech training is called *responsive* speech. This means that the parrot will reply to a statement or question. For example, the trainer asks, "You want a peanut?" and the macaw replies, "I sure do!" To teach the macaw responsive speech, first teach the bird the reply. Work on this until the macaw says the reply whenever you offer a reward. Then begin asking the bird the question and reward it for saying the reply. In this way you can teach the macaw many interesting responses to your statements. Acquisition of responsive speech takes longer than command speech, but it is worth the extra work if you have the time.

Training macaws to spread their wings on command is one of the author's responsibilities. At Parrot Jungle she trains the birds so well that other "trainers" can perform with the birds in front of thousands of people visiting Parrot Jungle in Miami every year (see facing page).

ADVANCED TRICK TRAINING

Macaws are natural acrobats. They are extremely intelligent and are capable of learning a variety of physical tricks. Their eyesight is keen enough to let you use color coding to teach the macaw to select one object from many similar objects. You can also teach the macaw to match objects of like shape and color.

The more physical tricks that you can teach include rolling over, lying on the back and playing dead, riding on a scooter and skates, walking on balls and tightropes and many other tricks. Use your imagination when deciding to teach your bird tricks.

The biggest obstacles to overcome are getting adequate props and finding enough time to teach the bird the tricks. The best props for the macaw are made of molded metal and have considerable weight. The weight gives the prop needed integrity; the macaw will not be able to use a prop that constantly falls over. Wood and plastic props do not hold up well. Some props can be purchased through pet supply dealers or bird clubs. The easiest way to come by good props is to design and build them yourself.

If you own a tame macaw and desire to attempt trick training, you must be prepared to give the bird a lesson at least once a day. The bird will not be able to learn anything if you do not give it at least one lesson a day. It is better to give frequent short lessons than one long lesson each day. If possible, give the bird a lesson once every hour for ten minutes. The frequent repetition will help the bird learn quickly.

Always have a reward available for the macaw whenever it responds correctly. Raw peanut bits work well. Praise the bird for correct responses.

Some tricks can be taught by rewarding for one behavior. Other tricks may have to be broken down into simple behaviors and taught in sequence. The first few lessons may be used to acclimate the macaw to the prop, because some birds shy away from strange toys or from the structured lesson itself. With these reluctant learners, be certain to keep the first few lessons very short. Don't force the parrot to attend for too long or the stressful situation will negatively reinforce the bird. Very short lessons of two or three minutes will help the bird accept the new routine more readily.

Always reward the bird immediately for correct responses. If you delay giving reinforcement the macaw will not be as motivated to work for you. Once the macaw has learned the basic behavior you can use delayed reinforcement to make the bird work more precisely, repeating the trick until you are satisfied. Then reward. Initially you just want the macaw to learn the basic behavior; then you can work closer and closer to the desired goal.

Never punish a macaw for giving an incorrect response. Simply withhold reinforcement until the bird responds correctly.

You can use visual or verbal signals to elicit responses from a macaw. The visual signal is more easily learned. Verbal signals take much longer. Auditory signals can also be used to cue responses from the bird.

Motivators that help the bird learn are affection, food reward and frequent attention in the form of trick training lessons. Do not starve your macaw to teach it tricks. Most macaws are bottomless and will always accept a food reward from their favorite trainer. House pets work more for attention and praise from their owner than they do for food reward.

EXAMPLE OF TRICK TRAINING

The task: to teach the bird to pick up colored rings and place them over matching pegs. Props include three rings (one yellow, one red and one blue) and also three pegs, also yellow, red and blue. First teach the bird to pick up a ring and give a reward for a successful performance. At first you may have to reward the bird for just touching the ring. Work with a ring and peg of only one color at a time.

Once the bird learns to pick up the ring every time and take a reward for it, move the peg closer to it and make the bird drop the ring on the peg. Reward. At first you may have to take the ring from the macaw and place it on the peg yourself. Still reward the macaw. It must associate seeing the ring on the peg with a reward. The peg should be present during the lesson even before you get to using it. Otherwise the bird may be shy at the sight of it.

Once the bird has mastered the behavior of picking up the ring and placing it on a peg with one colored set (yellow, let's say), go on to introduce the next color. Keep the first prop on the table while you work with a second color. Get the bird used to switching from one color to the other. Eventually try to confuse the macaw by giving it one ring and two differently colored pegs to choose from. Reward only for the correct choice. At first you will have to be active in helping the macaw make the correct choice. Soon the bird will distinguish the correct color for itself. This is the third behavior you have taught the macaw for one trick: to distinguish color and match it.

So the one trick encompassed three different behaviors. You taught them in sequence until the macaw learned the whole set. The first behavior was picking up the ring, the second was dropping the ring onto a peg, the third was discriminating color and matching it.

Some of the acts for which the author trains macaws. 1. The chariot race, where two macaws compete for speed. 2. Riding a truck by pumping the handle back and forth. 3. Flying onto her arm when the bird is called. Some birds are free to fly back to South America if they wish! 4. The intelligence test of separating colored rings and placing them on a rack according to their color.

The very rare Spix macaw, though very expensive, makes as good a pet as the blue and gold macaw on the facing page.

A FEW ADDITIONAL COMMENTS ON TRICK TRAINING

If you have decided to teach your macaw a trick, begin with something simple. It is important that the bird be successful in its first attempt at learning a trick. Build your bird's repertoire of tricks the same as you build its vocabulary. Work from the simple to the more complex.

Work on only one trick at a time. If you try to teach one trick but lose patience and begin on a second trick, you are going to confuse the macaw. In addition you are teaching the parrot that it is okay to be unsuccessful. This is a bad orientation if you plan to teach the bird many tricks. Once the bird has mastered one trick, spend two or three weeks letting it enjoy showing off before you begin teaching something new.

You must be consistent in your efforts to trick-train your macaw. If you work hard with the bird for three days and skip the next two you will be defeating the purpose. The bird will become frustrated and so will you, for the bird will never be able to learn.

An inconsistent trainer teaches the macaw to be an inconsistent performer. So if you do not really have the time to devote to formal trick training, stick to playing with the bird and hope that you can teach the bird a trick that does not rely upon props. Just handling the macaw can become a few simple tricks.

Macaws are popular birds for many reasons. They are intelligent,
come when they are called (as shown above), are very colorful and
are relatively abundant. Since they are large birds, they are popular
all over the world in bird shows, as seen by this demonstration of
"Go to sleep, little baby!" at the bird park in Honolulu.→

If you invest in a macaw, get the name of a local avian veterinarian in case of an emergency. When a bird is listless and sits continuously with its feathers puffed out, you can be sure you have a problem with an ill bird.

First Aid And Illness

It is a common accident for a macaw to break the tip of its beak and to lose some blood. If the bleeding is heavy you'll have to pack the wound to stop the bleeding.

You should get the name of an experienced avian veternarian when you first purchase the macaw. Keep the doctor's name, address and phone number in your personal phone directory.

In case of accidents, administer first aid and then call the vet for follow-up care. If you panic and rush the bird over to the vet, you may cause more harm to the bird and you may even find that the vet is not in.

The most common accidents that your macaw may have are breaking blood feathers and breaking claws or the tip of the beak. In all three situations the macaw will lose some blood. If just a few drops are noticed, do not panic. Leave the macaw to sit quietly to see whether the bleeding will stop by itself. If bleeding continues or accelerates, use styptic powder to stop it. Pack a small amount of powder into the bleeding spot. Hold the macaw until bleeding has abated and place it back in its cage for a rest. Keep an eye on the bird but don't bother it.

The broken blood feather may have to be pulled, but the primary need is to stop the bleeding. Have an experienced vet or bird handler pull the blood feather for you.

Open wounds should be cleaned with hydrogen peroxide and dressed with an antibiotic salve or powder. Have the vet examine the wound and give you the proper medication for dressing it. Do not try to cover open wounds. Macaws will not tolerate bandages; they soon tear them off.

Macaws love to bathe and, if the environment is warm, they should be allowed to bathe every day. After bathing they frequently sit with their wings held away from their bodies, as shown above, to allow their feathers to dry.

If your macaw takes a bad fall and you suspect that it has broken a bone, keep the bird warm and quiet until you can get to the vet. Don't examine the bird or you may cause more damage. It is best to keep the macaw in a small cage having a low perch and feed and water within easy reach.

The vet will probably want to X-ray the suspected break. Most often he will set the bone without splinting it. Then it is a matter of time and good diet to help the bird heal properly. Breaks may take from 7 to 12 weeks to heal completely, or they may heal much faster if not too severe. In any case, leave the bird in a small cage until you are certain that the break is healed. The vet may want to see the bird for repeat X-rays, a sure test to determine the state of healing.

Some broken bones break through the outer layer of skin. When this happens, be very careful to keep the macaw as still as possible. This is an emergency. Stop the bleeding and keep the bird warm and quiet. Call the vet immediately.

Concussion and shock resemble one another and should be treated similarly. Keep the macaw very warm and its vision restricted (to keep the bird calm). Place the bird in a small cage or box. If there is an open wound that is bleeding, administer first aid. Do not try to give the bird water; you may choke it. Do not rush the bird to the vet.

Shock is often the immediate cause of death in parrots, so learn to treat the symptoms yourself. Suspect shock when the macaw has suffered a bad fall or injury. The eyes do not dilate in response to light. The bird does not move and offers no resistance to your touching it. The breathing becomes shallow, and the bird feels clammy. It may make a soft moaning sound.

The bird may come out of shock quickly, but it may take a long time. Stay with the macaw to observe its recovery, but do not move it once you have placed it in a warm hospital cage or box.

Eye injuries should be treated by a veterinarian.

Macaws may catch cold and sneeze and cough just like people. When your macaw shows signs of a cold, be certain to see the vet.

A healthy macaw can throw off a simple cold with no bad after-effects. You must keep the bird warm and feed it an enriched diet. The vet may prescribe some antibiotic drugs to treat the cold. Do not try to dose out antibiotic drugs for the bird yourself. Improper drugs and dosages can give the bird a tolerance to antibiotics and not affect the disease at all. They may even kill the bird.

If left untreated, the simple cold can turn into a severe condition. Pneumonia and other respiratory diseases begin as colds. Intestinal ailments may begin as untreated or improperly treated colds. It is easier to prevent serious illness than to treat it.

Macaws may develop sinus trouble, which results in runny noses and eye problems. Again, see the vet for diagnosis and treatment.

Intestinal disorders may appear alone or be symptomatic of some other disorder. Sour crop is an intestinal disorder in which the bird cannot keep food down. It eats but regurgitates the food. The vet can give you an antacid for the bird or you can try giving it baking soda in water instead of plain water. Boil one quart of water and add one teaspoon of baking soda. Cool the mixture and give it to the bird as drinking water. You may also use Sal Hepatica, a mild laxative; it is sold at the drug store. Use one teaspoon of powder to one quart of boiled water. Cool and use for drinking water. Use for two to three days. If your macaw has other symptoms along with regurgitation, do not treat it for sour crop. See the vet as soon as possible.

Enteritis can be simple to treat when caught early, but if left untreated it can kill the macaw. The bird may have simple diarrhea or pass blood. See the vet immediately if you notice blood in the stool. Diarrhea and constipation may result from improper feeding. Check the diet and adjust if necessary. Sal Hepatica can be used to treat the constipation, but if the bird is not defecating within 24 hours, see the vet immediately. Use the same mixture of Sal Hepatica as for sour crop.

Most of the remaining ailments that are noteworthy are common to both macaws and humans. They result from environmental and genetic causes. They usually are a function of age. Macaws may develop cataracts in later life or as the result of traumatic injury. The high proportion of protein in their diet is a causal factor. That is why a diet of fruit and vegetables with sunflower and peanuts added is recommended for all macaws.

Macaws can suffer from overweight. This in turn can lead to heart disease and affect the other major organs. Macaws only develop orthopedic problems as they age. These diseases of aging must be treated with diet and sometimes with medicine. As with people, though, most macaws learn to live with their physical problems.

If your macaw eats a great deal and loses weight, see the vet. This may be due to parasite infestation (unusual with indoor pets) and must be treated by the vet.

Avian medicine is a very young field. Most surgeries performed on macaws are not routine. However, interested bird collectors sponsor research in avian medicine by seeking medical care for their pet parrots. Private people that find their pet parrot irreplaceable learn to keep it healthy with proper care and feeding and seek medical help if needed.

You can protect your pet from illness by feeding it properly and keeping it clean and in a good environment. Most macaws are very hardy birds and many never suffer from illness until age affects them.

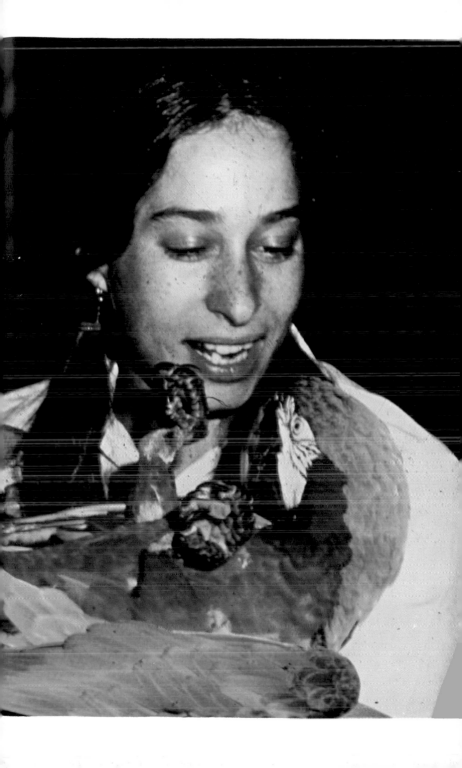

TAMING AND TRAINING
MACAWS
KW-054